COLLECTIONS

A Harcourt Reading / Language Arts Program

*Did you pack your
imagination? Your journeys
of wonder can begin now!*

Title Page

COLLECTIONS

A Harcourt Reading / Language Arts Program

JOURNEYS OF WONDER

SENIOR AUTHORS

Roger C. Farr • Dorothy S. Strickland • Isabel L. Beck

AUTHORS

Richard F. Abrahamson • Alma Flor Ada • Bernice E. Cullinan • Margaret McKeown • Nancy Roser
Patricia Smith • Judy Wallis • Junko Yokota • Hallie Kay Yopp

SENIOR CONSULTANT

Asa G. Hilliard III

CONSULTANTS

Karen S. Kutiper • David A. Monti • Angelina Olivares

Harcourt

Orlando   Boston   Dallas   Chicago   San Diego

Visit *The Learning Site!*

www.harcourtschool.com

JOURNEYS OF WONDER -x

Dear Reader,

Do you like to go places? You never know whom you might meet or what you might find out. Reading can be a way of going to new places.

In **Journeys of Wonder**, the stories, poems, and articles will take you to many exciting places. Some places are in the past, some are in outer space, and some are at the center of the Earth! You will meet many unusual characters and read about interesting facts. Some stories might even make you laugh out loud.

You can learn something new on every reading journey. As you read this book, you will learn to be a better reader. Reading is a journey that will last your whole life.

Fasten your seat belt, and open your eyes. Let's begin the journey right now.

Sincerely,

The Authors

The Authors

Tell Me a Story

CONTENTS

THEME

~ GOOD ~
NEIGHBORS

LEAH'S PONY

COCOA ICE
By DIANA APPELBAUM
Pictures by HOLLY MEADE

THE THREE
LITTLE JAVELINAS
By Susan Lowell
Illustrated by Jim Harris

IF YOU MADE
A MILLION
by David M. Schwartz
pictures by Steven Kellogg

DINER

CONTENTS

Celebrate Our World

Contents

THE
ARMADILLO
FROM
AMARILLO

LYNNE CHERRY

ROCKING AND
ROLLING
Philip Steele

Discover the awesome forces
that shape and move THE EARTH

ALEJANDRO'S GIFT
BY RICHARD E. ALBERT   ILLUSTRATED BY SYLVIA LONG

I'M IN CHARGE OF
CELEBRATIONS
by Byrd Baylor · pictures by Peter Parnall

KINGFISHER   YOUNG   DISCOVERERS
MAPS
AND
MAPPING
BARBARA TAYLOR

GEOGRAPHY FACTS AND EXPERIM

Using Reading Strategies

A strategy is a plan for doing something well.

You probably already use some strategies as you read. For example, you may **look at the title and pictures before you begin reading** a story. You may **think about what you want to find out while reading.** Using strategies like these can help you become a better reader.

Look at the list of strategies on page 9. You will learn about and use these strategies as you read the selections in this book. As you read, look back at the list to remind yourself of the **strategies good readers use.**

Strategies Good Readers Use

- Use Prior Knowledge
- Make and Confirm Predictions
- Adjust Reading Rate
- Self-Question
- Create Mental Images
- Use Context to Confirm Meaning
- Use Text Structure and Format
- Use Graphic Aids
- Use Reference Sources
- Read Ahead
- Reread
- Summarize

Here are some ways to check your own comprehension:

✔ Make a copy of this list on a piece of construction paper shaped like a bookmark.

✔ Have it handy as you read.

✔ After reading, talk with a classmate about which strategies you used and why.

Tell Me

CONTENTS

a Story

Reader's

The Wave
by Margaret Hodges

FOLKTALE

In this classic folktale, one man's courage and quick thinking save an entire Japanese village from ruin.

**Caldecott Honor;
ALA Notable Book
READER'S CHOICE LIBRARY**

What Do Authors Do?
by Eileen Christelow

NONFICTION

Take a peek inside an author's world! Find out how books are written and published.

**Notable Children's Book
in the Language Arts;
Booklist Editor's Choice
READER'S CHOICE LIBRARY**

Choice

The Tortoise and the Jackrabbit
by Susan Lowell

FABLE

In this twist on a familiar tale, the race is on between the tortoise and the jackrabbit!

The Malachite Palace
by Alma Flor Ada

FAIRY TALE

A yellow bird brings happiness to a lonely princess. When it stops singing, the princess finds a way to help.

Award-Winning Author

Papa Tells Chita a Story
by Elizabeth Fitzgerald Howard

HISTORICAL FICTION/TALL TALE

Chita loves to hear—and add to—her father's stories about the Spanish-American War in Cuba.

Notable Trade Book in Social Studies

Coyote
Places
the
Stars

retold and illustrated by
Harriet Peck Taylor

16

Many moons and many moons ago, a coyote lived in a canyon by a swift-running river. He spent his days roaming the land, chasing butterflies and sniffing wildflowers. He lay awake many nights gazing at the starry heavens.

One summer night, as he was relaxing in the cool grass with his friend Bear, Coyote had an idea. "I think I will climb to the heavens and discover their secrets!"

Bear scratched his big head and asked, "How can you do that?"

"I can get up there with no trouble at all," Coyote said.

Now, Coyote was very skillful with a bow and arrow. He gathered a very large pile of arrows and began to shoot them at the sky. The first arrow whistled through the air and landed on the moon. Coyote launched a second arrow, which caught in the notch of the first. *Whi-rr* went one arrow. *Whizz* went the next, and on and on until this long line of arrows made a ladder.

Coyote then began to climb. He climbed for many days and nights until he finally reached the moon. He slept all that day, as he was very tired.

That night Coyote had another clever idea. He wondered if he could move the stars around by shooting at them with his remaining arrows. His first arrow hit a star and moved it across the sky. He found he could place the stars wherever he wanted.

Coyote wagged his bushy tail and yelped for joy. He was going to make pictures in the sky for all the world to see.

First he decided to make a coyote, so he shot one arrow after another until the stars were arranged in the shape of a coyote. Next he thought of his friend Bear, and placed the stars in the form of a bear.

Coyote worked all night creating likenesses of all his
friends—Mountain Lion, Horse, Goat, Fish, Owl, and Eagle.
With the stars he had left over, he made a Big Road across
the sky. When he was finished, he began to descend his
ladder back to earth.

That night, when the bright moon rose in the
east, Coyote saw his handiwork and began to howl.
Oweowowooooah was carried on the wind through the
shadows of the canyon. Birds and animals awoke suddenly
and listened to the mysterious sound. It seemed to be
calling to them. From canyons and mesas, hills and plains
they came, following the sound.

Bears bounded out of their dens. Squirrels scampered and rabbits hippity-hopped over the hills. Bobcats crept and bristly porcupines waddled along the trail.

Graceful deer moved swiftly, while lizards slowly crawled across the desert.

Silvery fish splashed their way upstream. The mighty mountain lion and herds of buffalo joined the journey.

The great eagle soared over moonlit mountains. On and on went the parade of animals, following Coyote's magical voice.

Finally Coyote appeared, high on a rock. The animals formed a huge circle and all became quiet. Coyote's eyes blazed with pride as he said, "Animals and birds and all who are gathered here: Please look at the sky. You will see the stars are arranged in the shapes of animals. I made a ladder to the moon, and from there I shot my arrows to create the pictures you see."

As the animals looked up, a great chorus of whoofing and whiffing, screeching and squawking filled the air.

"I made a coyote and my friend Bear. You will see the mysterious Owl, the great Eagle, the Goat, Horse, Fish, and the mighty Mountain Lion. This is my handiwork, and I hope that all who see it will remember Coyote and all the animals of the canyon."

The animals gave a great feast for Coyote, and they sang and danced through the night. The animals decreed that Coyote was the most clever and crafty of all the animals.

Coyote was so grateful that he declared, "I will always be your friend and the friend of your children's children."

Now, to this day, if you listen closely in the still of the night as the moon is rising, you may even hear the magical howl of Coyote. He is calling you to go to your window, to gaze at the star pictures, and to dream.

Think About It

1. What did Coyote do to the stars in the night sky? Why did he do this?

2. What pictures would you have drawn with the stars?

3. How does this story explain why Coyote howls?

Meet the Author and Illustrator

Harriet Peck Taylor

Coyote Places the Stars was my first book. It is based on several Native American legends that explain the starry sky. During the time I was writing this book, I met a real coyote. Every day he would follow me on my daily hike. Sometimes the coyote would howl to me. One day I didn't see him, so I tried to make a wolf-like howl. To my surprise, he howled back and came out where I could see him. Seeing that coyote helped me paint the pictures for my book.

These illustrations are done with a type of painting called batik. Batik is an ancient artform that uses dyes and hot wax on cotton fabric.

 Visit *The Learning Site!*
www.harcourtschool.com

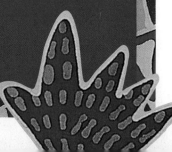

Response Activities

Meet Me at the Rock

WRITE AN ANNOUNCEMENT
The animals gather at the rock when they hear Coyote's howl. Suppose Coyote put an ad in a newspaper instead to announce the meeting. Write an announcement telling the animals why they should come to the meeting.

Star Pictures

DRAW A CONSTELLATION

Groups of stars that form pictures are called constellations. Learn the name and shape of one constellation from a book about the stars or an encyclopedia. Draw a dot-to-dot picture of the constellation. Invite a classmate to connect the dots to complete the picture.

Festival of Stars

WRITE A SONG

The animals sing and dance to celebrate Coyote's work. With a partner, write a song about the clever and crafty Coyote. You may use a tune you already know. Share your song with some classmates.

Thanks, Coyote!

WRITE A LETTER

The animals love Coyote's work. Write a thank-you letter from one of the animals to Coyote. Tell why you think the star pictures are a good idea. Decorate your letter with the star picture Coyote made of you.

Sequence

In "Coyote Places the Stars," Coyote makes plans and carries them out in order. Many stories are told in the order in which the events happen, or in **sequence.** Sometimes authors use time-order words such as **first, next, then, later,** and **finally.** These words let readers know the order in which things happen.

This diagram shows the sequence of events in "Coyote Places the Stars." You can use boxes and arrows like these to help you show when things happen in a story.

First, Coyote builds a ladder of arrows and climbs to the moon.

Next, he shoots arrows at the stars to make pictures of his animal friends.

Finally, the animals celebrate what Coyote has done.

Then, Coyote climbs down and calls all the animals to see his pictures in the sky.

When you read a story, think about the order in which things happen. This will help you understand the ideas and events that lead to the ending.

Watch for time-order words that give you clues.

Read the story below. What does Coyote do first, next, and last?

Snake was unhappy. "I don't see a star shape that looks like me," he said.

"I can fix that," said Coyote. First, he tied an arrow to a long, strong rope. Next, he shot the arrow into the sky and hooked it to a star. Then, he tugged hard on the rope. As the star tumbled toward Earth, it pulled a tail of fire behind it.

"It looks just like me!" cried Snake.

WHAT HAVE YOU LEARNED?

1. Reread one of your favorite stories. List some of the time-order words in the story that help you understand the sequence of events.

2. What might happen if the story events in "Coyote Places the Stars" were written out of sequence? Explain how this would be confusing.

Visit *The Learning Site!*
www.harcourtschool.com

TRY THIS • TRY THIS • TRY THIS

Think of a favorite game. What are some of the steps for playing this game? Write four steps in order.

> To play this game, this is what you do:
>
> 1. First,
> 2. Next,
> 3. Then,
> 4. Finally,

31

WHY MOSQUITOES BUZZ IN PEOPLE'S EARS

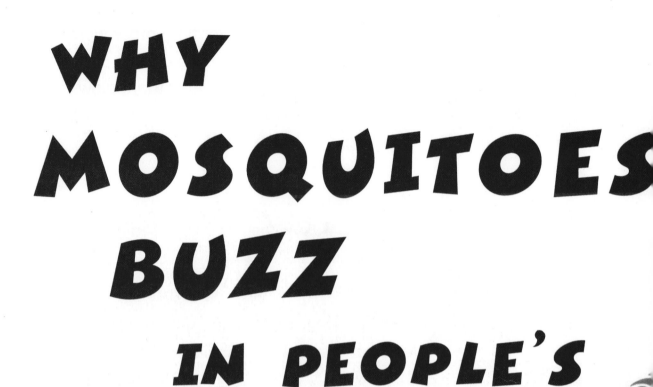

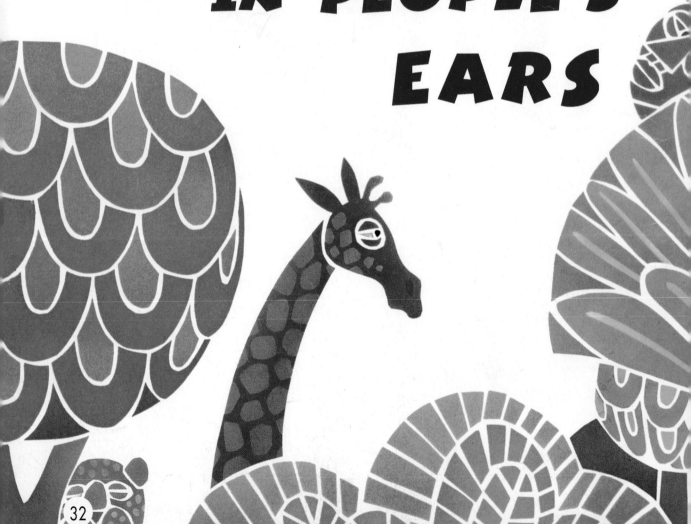

Why Mosquitoes Buzz In People's Ears
Verna Aardema | pictures by
Leo and Diane Dillon

Caldecott
Medal

A West African Tale
retold by
Verna Aardema
pictures by
Leo and
Diane Dillon

ONE MORNING a mosquito saw an iguana drinking at a waterhole. The mosquito said, "Iguana, you will never believe what I saw yesterday."

"Try me," said the iguana.

The mosquito said, "I saw a farmer digging yams that were almost as big as I am."

"What's a mosquito compared to a yam?" snapped the iguana grumpily. "I would rather be deaf than listen to such nonsense!" Then he stuck two sticks in his ears and went off, mek, mek, mek, mek, through the reeds.

The iguana was still grumbling to himself when he happened to pass by a python.

The big snake raised his head and said, "Good morning, Iguana."

The iguana did not answer but lumbered on, bobbing his head, badamin, badamin.

"Now, why won't he speak to me?" said the python to himself. "Iguana must be angry about something. I'm afraid he is plotting some mischief against me!" He began looking for somewhere to hide. The first likely place he found was a rabbit hole, and in it he went, wasawusu, wasawusu, wasawusu.

When the rabbit saw the big snake coming into her burrow, she was terrified. She scurried out through her back way and bounded, krik, krik, krik, across a clearing.

A crow saw the rabbit running for her life. He flew into the forest crying kaa, kaa, kaa! It was his duty to spread the alarm in case of danger.

A monkey heard the crow. He was sure that some dangerous beast was prowling near. He began screeching and leaping kili wili through the trees to help warn the other animals.

As the monkey was crashing through the treetops, he happened to land on a dead limb. It broke and fell on an owl's nest, killing one of the owlets.

Mother Owl was not at home. For though she usually hunted only in the night, this morning she was still out searching for one more tidbit to satisfy her hungry babies. When she returned to the nest, she found one of them dead. Her other children told her that the monkey had killed it. All that day and all that night, she sat in her tree—so sad, so sad, so sad!

Now it was Mother Owl who woke the sun each day so that the dawn could come. But this time, when she should have hooted for the sun, she did not do it.

The night grew longer and longer. The animals of the forest knew it was lasting much too long. They feared that the sun would never come back.

39

At last King Lion called a meeting of the animals. They came and sat down, pem, pem, pem, around a council fire. Mother Owl did not come, so the antelope was sent to fetch her.

When she arrived, King Lion asked, "Mother Owl, why have you not called the sun? The night has lasted long, long, long, and everyone is worried."

Mother Owl said, "Monkey killed one of my owlets. Because of that, I cannot bear to wake the sun."

The king said to the gathered animals:
"Did you hear?
  It was the monkey
  who killed the owlet —
  and now Mother Owl won't wake the sun
  so that the day can come."

Then King Lion called the monkey. He came before him nervously glancing from side to side, rim, rim, rim, rim.

"Monkey," said the king, "why did you kill one of Mother Owl's babies?"

"Oh, King," said the monkey, "it was the crow's fault. He was calling and calling to warn us of danger. And I went leaping through the trees to help. A limb broke under me, and it fell taaa on the owl's nest."

The king said to the council:
"So, it was the crow
  who alarmed the monkey,
  who killed the owlet —
  and now Mother Owl won't wake the sun
  so that the day can come."

Then the king called for the crow. That big bird came flapping up. He said, "King Lion, it was the rabbit's fault! I saw her running for her life in the daytime. Wasn't that reason enough to spread an alarm?"

The king nodded his head and said to the council:
"So, it was the rabbit
who startled the crow,
who alarmed the monkey,
who killed the owlet —
and now Mother Owl won't wake the sun
so that the day can come."

Then King Lion called the rabbit.
The timid little creature stood before him,
one trembling paw drawn up uncertainly.

"Rabbit," cried the king, "why did you
break a law of nature and go running,
running, running, in the daytime?"

"Oh, King," said the rabbit, "it was the
python's fault. I was in my house minding

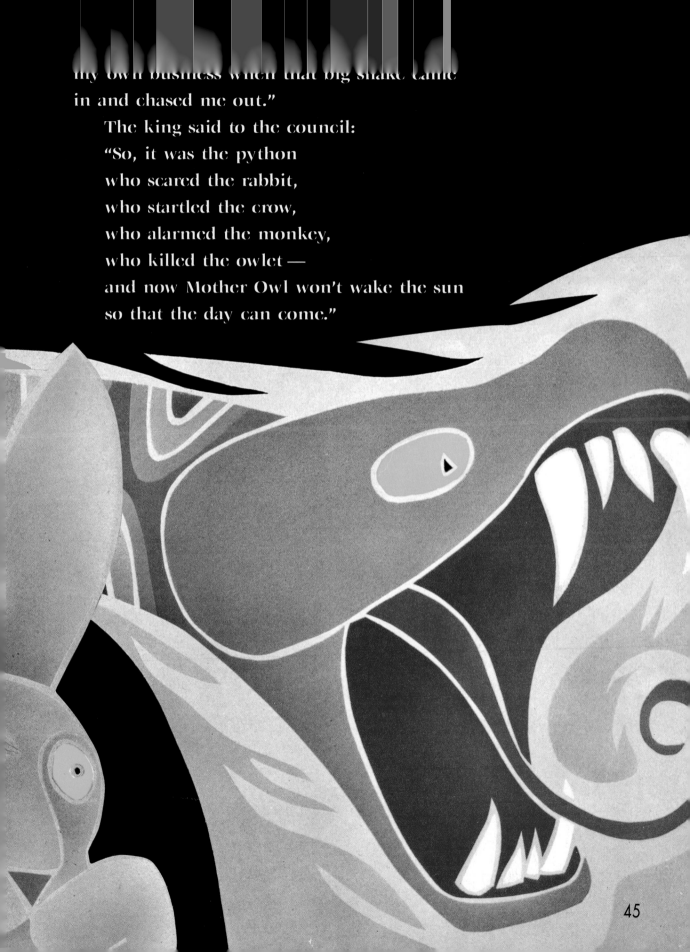

my own business when that big snake came
in and chased me out."

The king said to the council:
"So, it was the python
who scared the rabbit,
who startled the crow,
who alarmed the monkey,
who killed the owlet —
and now Mother Owl won't wake the sun
so that the day can come."

46

King Lion called the python, who came slithering, wasawusu, wasawusu, past the other animals. "But, King," he cried, "it was the iguana's fault! He wouldn't speak to me. And I thought he was plotting some mischief against me. When I crawled into the rabbit's hole, I was only trying to hide."

The king said to the council:
"So, it was the iguana
who frightened the python,
who scared the rabbit,
who startled the crow,
who alarmed the monkey,
who killed the owlet —
and now Mother Owl won't wake the sun
so that the day can come."

Now the iguana was not at the meeting. For he had not heard the summons.

The antelope was sent to fetch him.

All the animals laughed when they saw the iguana coming, badamin, badamin, with the sticks still stuck in his ears!

King Lion pulled out the sticks, purup, purup. Then he asked, "Iguana, what evil have you been plotting against the python?"

"None! None at all!" cried the iguana. "Python is my friend!"

"Then why wouldn't you say good morning to me?" demanded the snake.

I didn't hear you, or even see you," said the iguana. "Mosquito told me such a big lie, I couldn't bear to listen to it. So I put sticks in my ears."

"Nge, nge, nge," laughed the lion. "So that's why you had sticks in your ears!"

"Yes," said the iguana. "It was the mosquito's fault."

King Lion said to the council:
"So, it was the mosquito
who annoyed the iguana,
who frightened the python,
who scared the rabbit,

50

who startled the crow,
who alarmed the monkey,
who killed the owlet—
and now Mother Owl won't wake the sun
so that the day can come."

"Punish the mosquito! Punish the mosquito!"
cried all the animals.
    When Mother Owl heard that, she was satisfied.
She turned her head toward the east and hooted:
"Hoo! Hooooo! Hooooooo!"
    And the sun came up.

Meanwhile the mosquito had listened to it all from a nearby bush. She crept under a curly leaf, *semm*, and was never found and brought before the council.

But because of this the mosquito has a guilty conscience. To this day she goes about whining in people's ears: "Zeee! Is everyone still angry at me?"

When she does that, she gets an honest answer.

KPAO!

THINK ABOUT IT

1 How did the iguana's actions cause Mother Owl not to wake the sun?

2 What would you have done differently if the mosquito had told you the yam story?

3 What kind of tale is this? Why do you think it is still being told today?

MEET THE ILLUSTRATORS

LEO AND DIANE DILLON

Leo and Diane Dillon have been working as a team for more than thirty years! They are married and work in New York City. But what did they do before they were a team?

When Leo Dillon was a boy, he drew pictures of everything he saw. Although his parents encouraged him to draw, they hoped he would become a lawyer or doctor. Unlike her husband, Diane Dillon didn't always want to be an artist. She thought about becoming a nurse. After taking a few art lessons, she decided to go to art school. That is where she met Leo Dillon.

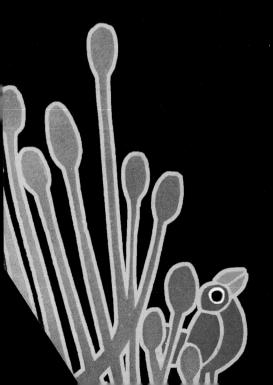

The Dillons have worked together on book covers, magazines, posters, and children's books. When working on a picture together, they pass the drawing back and forth between them. They each draw one small section at a time. Their work has won them many awards, including two Caldecott Medals in a row!

Leo Dillon

Diane Dillon

Visit *The Learning Site!*
www.harcourtschool.com

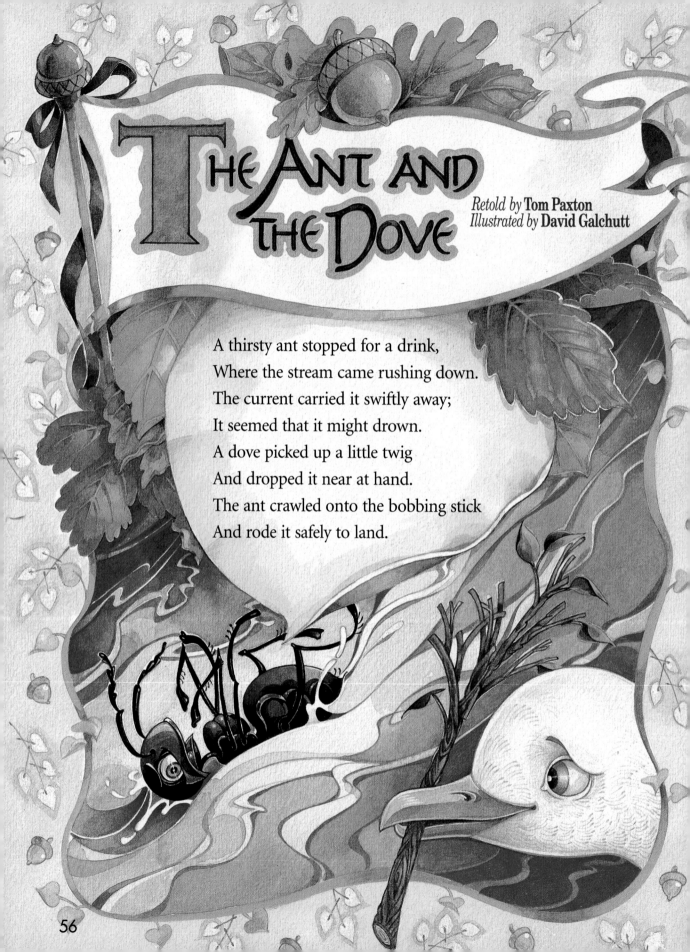

The Ant and the Dove

Retold by **Tom Paxton**
Illustrated by **David Galchutt**

A thirsty ant stopped for a drink,
Where the stream came rushing down.
The current carried it swiftly away;
It seemed that it might drown.
A dove picked up a little twig
And dropped it near at hand.
The ant crawled onto the bobbing stick
And rode it safely to land.

Later a hunter was setting a trap—
The dove would be his prey.
The ant crept up and stung his leg,
And the hunter ran away.
Remember, sister!
Remember, brother!
One good turn deserves another.

Think About It

Why is the friendship between
the ant and the dove unusual?

RESPONSE ACTIVITIES

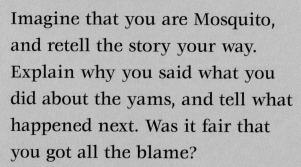

MOSQUITO SPEAKS

TELL A STORY

Imagine that you are Mosquito, and retell the story your way. Explain why you said what you did about the yams, and tell what happened next. Was it fair that you got all the blame?

HERE'S WHY

CREATE A POURQUOI TALE

The French word *pourquoi* means "why." This story explains why mosquitoes buzz in people's ears. Make up a story that explains something else. You might tell why tigers have stripes, why crickets chirp, or why moles live underground. Then act out your story with some classmates.

WEST AFRICA TODAY
WRITE A REPORT
This story comes from West Africa. With a partner, find out more about this part of Africa. What countries make up West Africa today? What do people there do for a living? What animals live in this part of Africa? Write a report about what you learn.

MAKING CONNECTIONS
WRITE A STORY
What if the ant and the dove met the mosquito from "Why Mosquitoes Buzz in People's Ears"? What would they say to each other? Write a new story. Tell what the ant and the dove might say to the mosquito about how to treat others.

A BOOKWORM WHO HATCHED

by
Verna Aardema
Photographs by Dede Smith

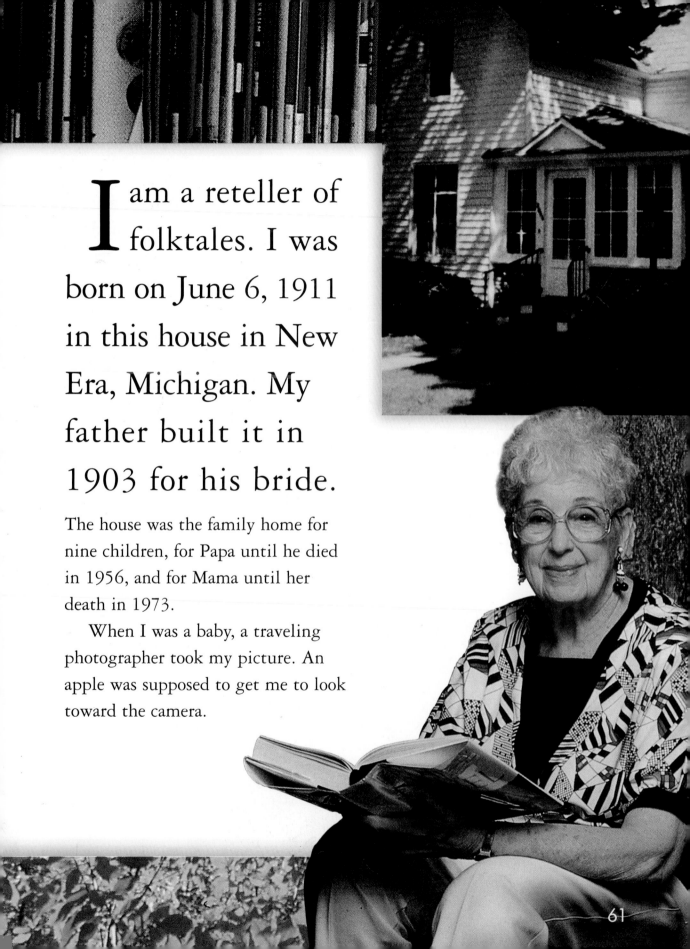

I am a reteller of folktales. I was born on June 6, 1911 in this house in New Era, Michigan. My father built it in 1903 for his bride.

The house was the family home for nine children, for Papa until he died in 1956, and for Mama until her death in 1973.

When I was a baby, a traveling photographer took my picture. An apple was supposed to get me to look toward the camera.

The next year, a traveling man photographed the first four children: Lawrence, 4, Evelyn, 6, me, 2, and Baby Sally. After this, either no photographer ever came to our door or our mother was too busy to let one in. The five children who came later were sorry about that.

For me, becoming a writer probably began with loving stories. Mama read to us children as we sprawled on the floor around her rocking chair—me near the back so I could hide with my tears if the story was sad. My first very own book was *Hans Andersen's Fairy Tales*. In my small rocking chair at bedtime, I would read "The Little Mermaid." After finishing the story in tears because of the sad ending I'd crawl into bed with my little sister Sally.

We children loved to act out stories. Mama let us play with her wedding dress. It was the inspiration for many a show which we and our friends put on upstairs in the carriage house. It was all we needed to create a folklore princess or a Sleeping Beauty.

A cedar swamp back of our homes was my and my cousin Elaine's special domain. In it we explored patches of wild flowers and squawberries. We climbed trees to peep into robins' nests. And we visited our *secret room*. That was a cave-like space inside a clump of trees. It was carpeted with black swamp soil and our furniture was a fallen log.

Great Grandfather VanderVen

Eric Norberg Magdelena Martin VanderVen Gertrude

Alfred Norberg Dora VanderVen

Evelyn Lawrence Marcella Dorothy Candace Stanley Austin Melva

Albert Aardema Verna Joel Vogteveen

Adele Austin Paula Dennis

Jill Chuck Alan Kris Dan Stevie

One day, when I was an eleven-year-old, "nose-in-the-book" bookworm, Mama read a poem I had written and she said, "Why, Verna, you're going to be a writer just like my Grandpa VanderVen." At once I decided to make writing my career.

After that, to escape having to help with the dishes I would run off to the swamp. Alone in my dark *secret room* I would sit and think and think until I thought my sisters must be finished with the dishes. That's when I made up my first stories. Soon, I began writing down the stories I thought of in the swamp and asking God to help me to become a good writer.

In high school I wrote school news for the paper. At Michigan

State College I took all of the writing courses. I began my writing career as a staff correspondent for *The Muskegon Chronicle*. My first husband, Albert Aardema, was as happy as I to see "By Verna Aardema" at the top of a story.

Our little daughter, Paula, got me started writing for children. I had to make up stories to get her to eat. I mailed a "feeding story" about Africa to a publisher. The editor suggested that I use it as chapter one of a juvenile novel. I did African folktales instead. And *Tales from the Story Hat* was born.

The bookworm I was had hatched. I was an author! I have published more than 25 books.

Because I retell folktales, I have to start with an authentic tale. One day a college student from Nigeria, West Africa, came to our house. He told us a traditional tale his grandmother had told him when he was a child.

I usually find the tales I retell in old books, obtained for me through interlibrary loan. By computer, librarian Ann Fields locates and requests the source book I ask for. She uses codes for the title and for the author.

After finding a folktale I like and deciding how I want to redo it (tell it in my own words), I write it first in pencil. Then, using the typewriter, I revise it at least three times.

Then it goes to my agent and she forwards it to the editor. If the editor buys the story she helps me to perfect it. Then the type is set. The many corrections on this galley proof show what happened when by mistake, the first version instead of the final revision was sent to the typesetter.

Next, an illustrator is chosen to do the pictures. The illustrator cannot *tell* the editor what he plans to do. He has to *show* her!

Borreguita and the Coyote
A Tale from Ayutla
Mexico

On a farm at the foot of a mountain ~~in Mexico~~, there once lived a little ewe lamb. Her master called her simply *Borreguita*, which means "little lamb."

One day Borreguita's master tied her to a stake in an alfalfa field. a/red The lamb was eating the lush green plants when a coyote came along.

The coyote ~~said~~ "Borreguita, I'm going to eat you!" growled "Grrr!/

Borreguita bleated, "BA-A-A, BA-A-A! ~~Oh~~ Señor Coyote, I would not fill you up. I am thin as a bean pod. When I have eaten all this alfalfa, I shall be fat. You may eat me then." clover Caps

Coyote looked at the skinny little lamb and the wide alfalfa field. clover "Está bien. That is good," he said. "When you are fat, I shall come back."

After many days the coyote returned. He found the lamb grazing in a meadow. He ~~said~~ "Borreguita, you are as plump as a growled "Grrr!/ tumbleweed. I'm going to eat you now!"

"Señor Coyote," ~~cried Borreguita~~, "I know something that tastes ever so much better than lamb!"

"What?" asked Coyote.

"Cheese!" cried Borreguita. "My master keeps a round of cheese on his table. He eats it on his tacos."

The coyote had never heard of cheese, and he was curious about it. "How can I get some of this cheese?" he asked.

Borreguita said, "There is a pond at the end of the pasture. Tonight, when the moon is high, meet me there. And I will show you how to get a cheese."

"Está bien," said Coyote. "I will be there."

That night, when the full moon was straight up in the sky, Borreguita and Coyote met at the edge of the pond.

There, glowing in the black water, was something that looked like for all the world a big, round cheese.

"Do you see it?" cried Borreguita. "Swim out and get it."

Coyote slipped into the water and paddled toward the cheese. He shuh, shuk, swam and swam, but the cheese stayed just so far ahead. Finally, he opened his mouth and lunged—WHOOSH!

67

So he makes book dummies. This is one which Will Hillenbrand made for my *Traveling to Tondo*. He made it of paper and cardboard.

Will says, "I think in pictures." On a letter to me he drew what he saw in his mind for a bookworm who hatched.

Finally, the story goes to the printer. Eventually, the day comes when the book which began as a code on the OCLC (Online Computer Library Center) computer comes off the press and my advance copies arrive!

My first husband Al had died in 1974, and the next year I married Joel Vugteveen, who had grown up with me in New Era. In 1984 we

moved to southwestern Florida to be near my son Austin. Early mornings are cool and lovely here. Often I'm out picking up the paper before the stars have dimmed. I read the news and do the Jumble puzzle while I eat my breakfast. Joel and I like to swim and to bicycle around the park.

When our children and grandchildren come to visit, I often bake a pie for dessert. Making a tasty pie is as important as writing a good story, I think, and you can't *eat* a story!

Stevie is my youngest grandchild. He likes to stay at our house for a few days at a time. He is a bookworm, too.

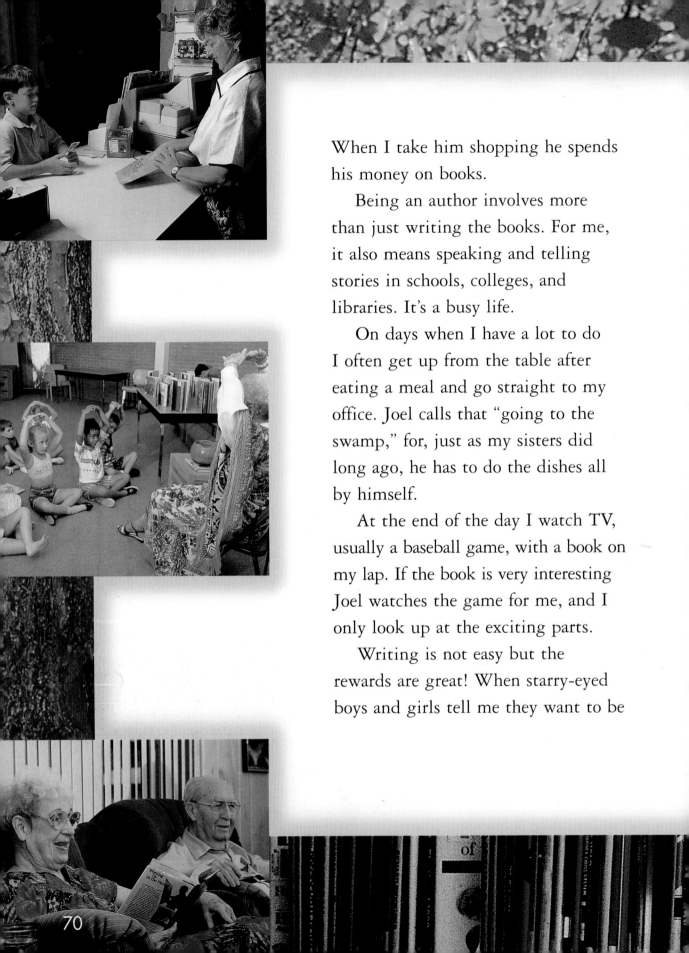

When I take him shopping he spends his money on books.

Being an author involves more than just writing the books. For me, it also means speaking and telling stories in schools, colleges, and libraries. It's a busy life.

On days when I have a lot to do I often get up from the table after eating a meal and go straight to my office. Joel calls that "going to the swamp," for, just as my sisters did long ago, he has to do the dishes all by himself.

At the end of the day I watch TV, usually a baseball game, with a book on my lap. If the book is very interesting Joel watches the game for me, and I only look up at the exciting parts.

Writing is not easy but the rewards are great! When starry-eyed boys and girls tell me they want to be

authors, I hug them for success.
One of them later wrote to me,
"When I become an author and visit
schools, I'll tell them that you
hugged me and I owe it all to you."

THINK ABOUT IT

1 What is Verna Aardema's life as a
writer like?

2 The author says that she went to a
secret place to think of ideas for stories.
What helps you think of ideas?

3 How can you tell the author likes
being a writer and a storyteller?

RESPONSE ACTIVITIES

CHANGE PLACES

REWRITE A TALE

The folktales Verna Aardema retells come from Africa. She wants them to sound like stories told in that part of the world. Other storytellers may change the setting of a tale. Choose a folktale you know well. Rewrite it so that the story takes place in your state. How would the people or animals be different?

SECRET PLACE

WRITE A DESCRIPTION

When Verna Aardema was young, the swamp was her special writing place. What special writing place would you choose? Would it be the top room of a castle, a cozy mountain cabin, or some other place? Write a paragraph that describes your secret place.

THINKING IN PICTURES

DRAW A STORY

The artist, Will Hillenbrand, tells Verna Aardema that he "thinks in pictures." To try this, think of a folktale you and your classmates know. Then tell the story using only pictures. Make sure you draw the events in the correct order. Can your classmates guess what story you have shown?

BOOK STORY

MAKE A FLOWCHART

Verna Aardema describes the steps in putting a book together. With a partner, make a flowchart that shows how one of her stories becomes a book. Start with the "authentic tale." Use arrows to show how one event leads to the next. Finish with the author getting the first copy.

FOCUS SKILL Fact and Opinion

In "A Bookworm Who Hatched," Verna Aardema gives many facts about her life. She also shares some of her opinions. A **fact** is a statement that can be checked or proven. An **opinion** tells what someone thinks or feels. You can use a chart like the one below to help you decide if a statement is a fact or an opinion.

Fact or Opinion?

Is It a Fact?

- Can it be proven?
- Could someone show that it is true or not true?

Is It an Opinion?

- Does it tell a person's feelings?
- Does the writer use words that show feelings, such as **good** or **bad**?

Examples from the Selection

- The house was the family home for nine children.
- I read the news and do the Jumble puzzle while I eat my breakfast.

Examples from the Selection

- Early mornings are cool and lovely here.
- Making a tasty pie is as important as writing a good story, I think.

Sometimes writers give their opinions as if they were facts. It is important to be able to tell the difference between facts and opinions so you can form your own ideas about things you read.

Read the newspaper article below. Which statements are facts, and which are opinions? How does the writer of the article want you to feel about the new bookstore?

New Bookstore Opens

Tuesday at 9:00 A.M. a new store called Bookland opened on Main Street. The store is a perfect addition to downtown. It has thousands of books on many different subjects. Customers will enjoy the cozy chairs and the pretty posters on the walls. The store is beautifully decorated, and the prices are good.

WHAT HAVE YOU LEARNED?

1 Julie says that each person in her class wrote a poem. Tamika says that writing poetry is fun. Which is a fact? Which is an opinion? How do you know?

2 Read a short article in a newspaper or magazine. List some of the facts and opinions from the article.

TRY THIS ● TRY THIS ● TRY THIS

Think of a song you have heard or a movie you have seen. Write three facts about it. Then write your opinion of it.

Visit *The Learning Site!*
www.harcourtschool.com

75

Cloudy With a
Meat

written by Judi Barrett
drawn by Ron Barrett

Chance of balls

Cloudy With a Chance of Meatballs

77

We were all sitting around the big kitchen table. It was Saturday morning. Pancake morning. Mom was squeezing oranges for juice. Henry and I were betting on how many pancakes we each could eat. And Grandpa was doing the flipping.

Seconds later, something flew through the air headed toward the kitchen ceiling . . . and landed right on Henry.

After we realized that the flying object was only a pancake, we all laughed, even Grandpa. Breakfast continued quite uneventfully Z. All the other pancakes landed in the pan. And all of them were eaten, even the one that landed on Henry.

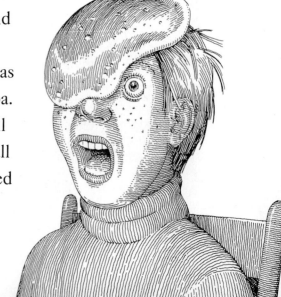

That night, touched off by the pancake incident at breakfast, Grandpa told us the best tall-tale bedtime story he'd ever told.

"Across an ocean, over lots of huge bumpy mountains, across three hot deserts, and one smaller ocean . . . there lay the tiny town of Chewandswallow.

In most ways, it was very much like any other tiny town. It had a Main Street lined with stores, houses with trees and gardens around them, a schoolhouse, about three hundred people, and some assorted cats and dogs.

But there were no food stores in the town of Chewandswallow. They didn't need any. The sky supplied all the food they could possibly want.

The only thing that was really different about Chewandswallow was its weather. It came three times a day, at breakfast, lunch, and dinner. Everything that everyone ate came from the sky.

Whatever the weather served, that was what they ate.

But it never rained rain. It never snowed snow. And it never blew just wind. It rained things like soup and juice. It snowed mashed potatoes and green peas. And sometimes the wind blew in storms of hamburgers.

The people could watch the weather report on television in the morning and they would even hear a prediction for the next day's food.

When the townspeople went outside, they carried their plates, cups, glasses, forks, spoons, knives and napkins with them. That way they would always be prepared for any kind of weather.

If there were leftovers, and there usually were, the people took them home and put them in their refrigerators in case they got hungry between meals.

The menu varied.

By the time they woke up in the morning, breakfast was coming down.

After a brief shower of orange juice, low clouds of sunny-side up eggs moved in followed by pieces of toast. Butter and jelly sprinkled down for the toast. And most of the time it rained milk afterwards.

For lunch one day, frankfurters, already in their rolls, blew in from the northwest at about five miles an hour.

There were mustard clouds nearby. Then the wind shifted to the east and brought in baked beans.

A drizzle of soda finished off the meal.

Dinner one night consisted of lamb chops, becoming heavy at times, with occasional ketchup. Periods of peas and baked potatoes were followed by gradual clearing, with a wonderful Jell-O setting in the west.

The Sanitation Department of Chewandswallow had a rather unusual job for a sanitation department. It had to remove the food that fell on the houses and sidewalks and lawns. The workers cleaned things up after every meal and fed all the dogs and cats. Then they emptied some of it into the surrounding oceans for the fish and turtles and whales to eat. The rest of the food was put back into the earth so that the soil would be richer for the people's flower gardens.

Life for the townspeople was delicious until the weather took a turn for the worse.

One day there was nothing but Gorgonzola cheese all day long.

The next day there was only broccoli, all overcooked.

And the next day there were brussel sprouts and peanut butter with mayonnaise.

Another day there was a pea soup fog. People could not see where they were going and they could barely find the rest of the meal that got stuck in the fog.

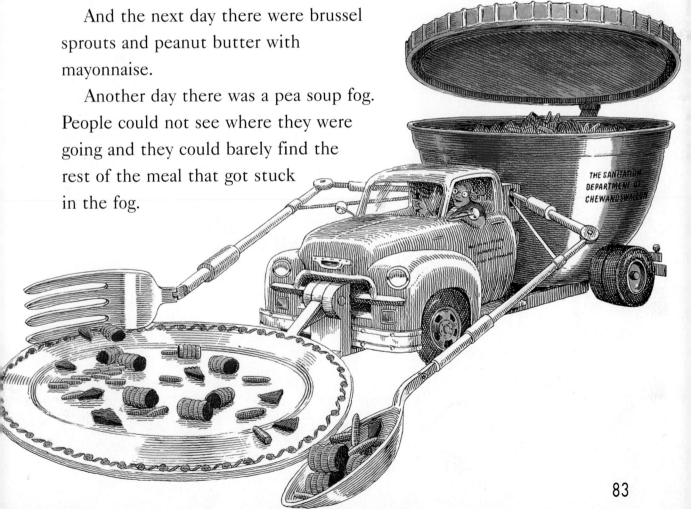

THE SANITATION DEPARTMENT OF CHEWANDSWALLOW

The food was getting larger and larger, and so were the portions. The people were getting frightened. Violent storms blew up frequently. Awful things were happening.

One Tuesday there was a hurricane of bread and rolls all day long and into the night. There were soft rolls and hard rolls, some with seeds and some without. There was white bread and rye and whole wheat toast. Most of it was larger than they had ever seen bread and rolls before. It was a terrible day. Everyone had to stay indoors. Roofs were damaged, and the Sanitation Department was beside itself. The mess took the workers four days to clean up, and the sea was full of floating rolls.

To help out, the people piled up as much bread as they could in their backyards. The birds picked at it a bit, but it just stayed there and got staler and staler.

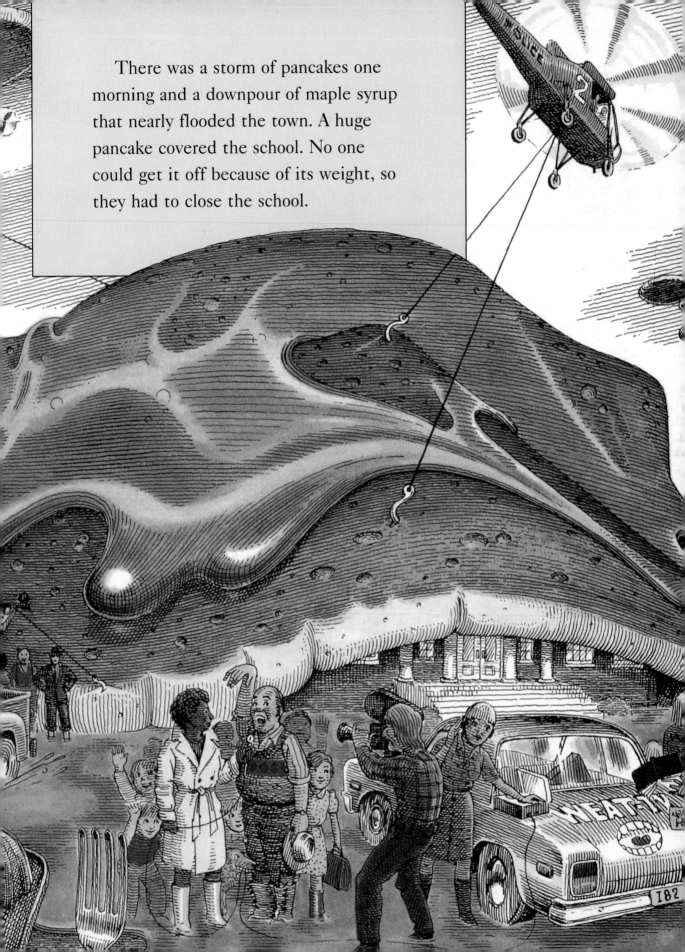

There was a storm of pancakes one morning and a downpour of maple syrup that nearly flooded the town. A huge pancake covered the school. No one could get it off because of its weight, so they had to close the school.

Lunch one day brought fifteen-inch drifts of cream cheese and jelly sandwiches. People ate themselves sick and the day ended with a stomachache.

There was an awful salt and pepper wind accompanied by an even worse tomato tornado. People were sneezing themselves silly and running to avoid the tomatoes. The town was a mess. There were seeds and pulp everywhere.

The Sanitation Department gave up. The job was too big.

People feared for their lives. They couldn't go outside most of the time. Many houses had been badly damaged by giant meatballs, stores were boarded up and there was no more school for the children.

So a decision was made to abandon the town of Chewandswallow.

It was a matter of survival.

The people glued together the giant pieces of stale bread sandwich-style with peanut butter, took the absolute necessities with them, and set sail on their rafts for a new land.

After being afloat for a week, they finally reached a small coastal town, which welcomed them. The bread had held up surprisingly well, well enough for them to build temporary houses for themselves out of it.

The children began school again, and the adults all tried to find places for themselves in the new land. The biggest change they had to make was getting used to buying food at a supermarket. They found it odd that the food was kept on shelves, packaged in boxes, cans and bottles. Meat that had to be cooked was kept in large refrigerators. Nothing came down from the sky except rain and snow. The clouds above their heads were not made of fried eggs. No one ever got hit by a hamburger again.

And nobody dared to go back to Chewandswallow to find out what had happened to it. They were too afraid."

Henry and I were awake until the very end of Grandpa's story. I remember his goodnight kiss.

The next morning we woke up to see snow falling outside our window.

We ran downstairs for breakfast and ate it a little faster than usual so we could go sledding with Grandpa.

It's funny, but even as we were sliding down the hill we thought we saw a giant pat of butter at the top, and we could almost smell mashed potatoes.

Think About It

1. How is Chewandswallow like a real town? How is it different?

2. Would you like to live in a place where it rains food and juice? Explain your answer.

3. How can you tell that the story Grandpa tells the children is a tall tale?

Meet the Author
Judi Barrett

As you can see from reading "Cloudy With a Chance of Meatballs," Judi Barrett is a wonderful storyteller. "I like to play with words," she says. She uses her imagination, mostly, and hardly ever writes about things that happen to her or to the people she knows.

Judi started making up stories when she was quite young. In the third grade, she wrote a story about a coin that came to life. To make the story itself come to life, she made a coin out of cardboard and added arms and legs! Making props for her stories was another way Judi used her imagination.

Judi Barrett has advice for young writers. "Read a lot," she says. "Keep writing and save your ideas. You may be able to use them later."

Meet the Illustrator
Ron Barrett

Ron Barrett was born in New York. He still lives and works there today. He studied art at the Pratt Institute in Brooklyn, New York, and he worked as an art director for the Children's Television Network.

When Ron Barrett draws food, he eats it! In order to illustrate one book, he ate things like strawberry shortcake, broccoli, and potato chips. You might guess that when he drew the pictures for "Cloudy With a Chance of Meatballs," he ate a lot of food! He says all this eating helps him draw.

Ron Barrett has won many awards for his artwork. His work has been shown at famous museums, including the Louvre in Paris.

Visit *The Learning Site!*
www.harcourtschool.com

91

Response Activities

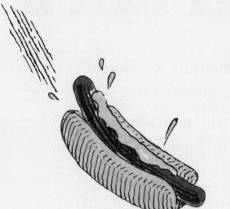

Weather Report
GIVE AN ANNOUNCEMENT

You are a TV weather reporter in the town of Chewandswallow, and your favorite meal is on the way! Give a weather report telling viewers what meal is coming. Also tell them what they might need to take outside to catch the food.

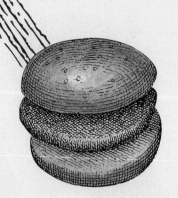

No School Today
DESCRIBE AN EVENT

Bad weather sometimes causes schools and businesses to close. Imagine that you are staying at home because of a storm. Write about what the weather is like and how you feel about missing school.

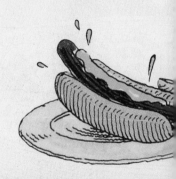

Another Whopper
TELL A TALL TALE

Grandpa tells a tall tale about the town of Chewandswallow. Make up your own story about a town where impossible things happen. Give your town a name. Tell a tall tale about something that happens there.

Food Facts
MAKE A POSTER

Find fun facts about your favorite foods. For example, how large was the largest tomato ever grown? How big was the biggest pizza? Use an almanac or the *Guinness Book of World Records* to find out. Make a poster about one fun food fact.

THE CROWDED HOUSE

BY EVA JACOB
ILLUSTRATED BY HOLLY COOPER

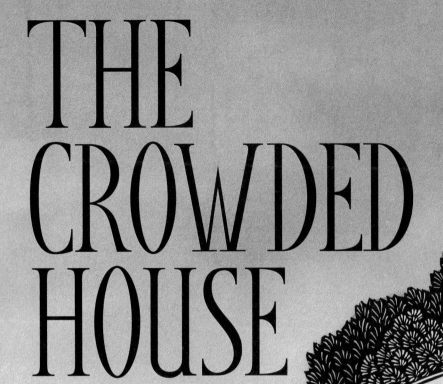

CHARACTERS

FATHER, *John the Carpenter*

MOTHER

MOLLY

JOAN

MEG

MARY ANN

MARTIN

WILLY

TOM

JOSEPH

GRANNY

BARTHOLOMEW, *the Wise Man*

GOAT

6 CHICKENS

DONKEY

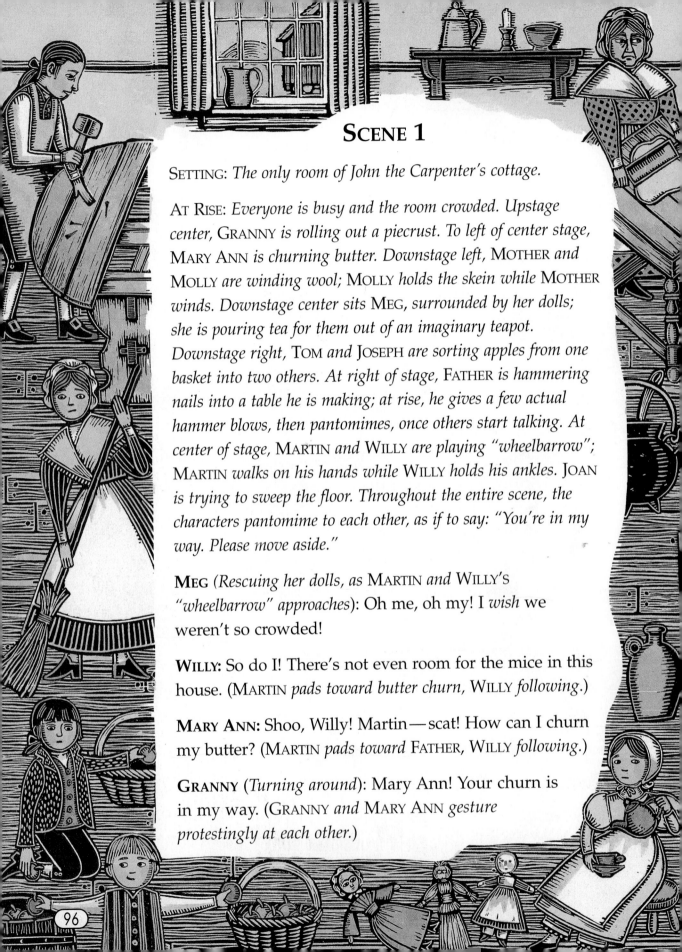

Scene 1

Setting: *The only room of John the Carpenter's cottage.*

At Rise: *Everyone is busy and the room crowded. Upstage center,* Granny *is rolling out a piecrust. To left of center stage,* Mary Ann *is churning butter. Downstage left,* Mother *and* Molly *are winding wool;* Molly *holds the skein while* Mother *winds. Downstage center sits* Meg, *surrounded by her dolls; she is pouring tea for them out of an imaginary teapot. Downstage right,* Tom *and* Joseph *are sorting apples from one basket into two others. At right of stage,* Father *is hammering nails into a table he is making; at rise, he gives a few actual hammer blows, then pantomimes, once others start talking. At center of stage,* Martin *and* Willy *are playing "wheelbarrow";* Martin *walks on his hands while* Willy *holds his ankles.* Joan *is trying to sweep the floor. Throughout the entire scene, the characters pantomime to each other, as if to say: "You're in my way. Please move aside."*

Meg (*Rescuing her dolls, as* Martin *and* Willy's *"wheelbarrow" approaches*): Oh me, oh my! I *wish* we weren't so crowded!

Willy: So do I! There's not even room for the mice in this house. (Martin *pads toward butter churn,* Willy *following.*)

Mary Ann: Shoo, Willy! Martin—scat! How can I churn my butter? (Martin *pads toward* Father, Willy *following.*)

Granny (*Turning around*): Mary Ann! Your churn is in my way. (Granny *and* Mary Ann *gesture protestingly at each other.*)

FATHER (*To* MARTIN *and* WILLY): Children, don't play here. There isn't any room.

JOAN (*Pausing with broom in front of apple baskets*): Joseph! Tom! Please move aside. How can I sweep? (BOYS *carrying baskets move angrily toward Meg.*)

MEG (*Again rescuing dolls*): No, Tom, you mustn't sit here. You're right in the middle of my tea party! (MEG, TOM, *and* JOSEPH *pantomime a quarrel. Others all begin talking at once.*)

ALL: You're in my way. Please move over. How can I work? There's no room in this house! Why must we be so crowded?

FATHER (*At the top of his lungs*): Quiet! Be still, I say. (*Others are silent.* FATHER *clutches his head.*) Oh my ears and shoe buttons! All this noise! You'll drive me out of my wits! (*A knock is heard at door left.*)

MOTHER: Husband, I hear a knock at the door. (*Knock is repeated.*)

FATHER: Aye, good wife. I hear it. (*Loudly*) Come in.

BARTHOLOMEW (*Entering. Leans on his staff and bows*): Good day to you, my friends.

GRANNY: Why, 'tis Wise Bartholomew himself!

BARTHOLOMEW (*Bowing again*): None other.

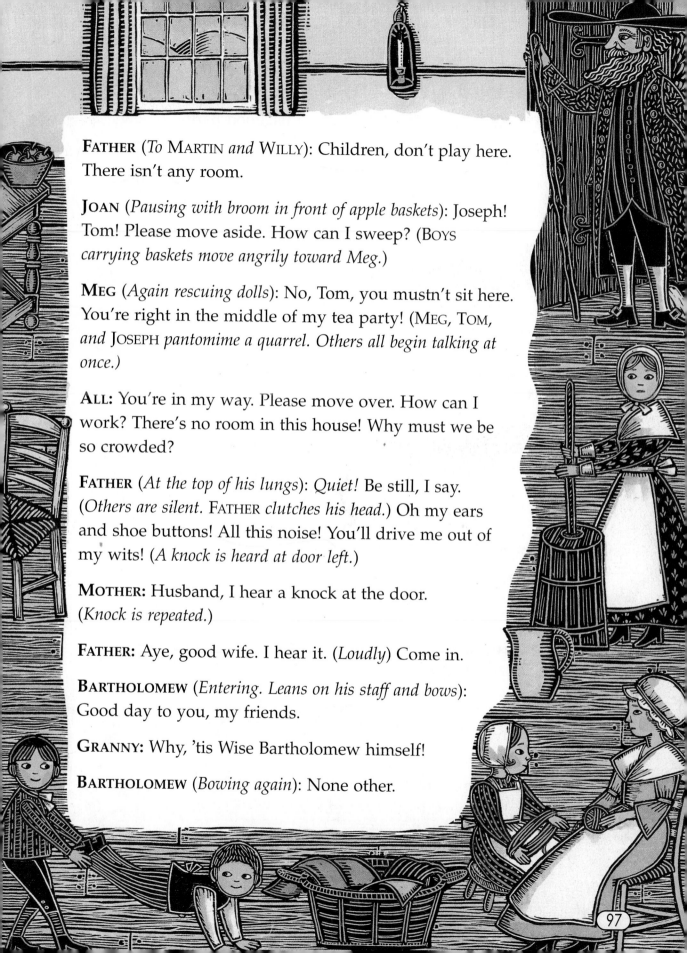

MOLLY: Have you come to visit us, good Bartholomew?

BARTHOLOMEW: Nay, my child. I was on my way to the forest, but I heard such a shouting and wailing in this house that I thought there must be some trouble.

MOTHER (*Wiping her eyes with her apron*): Alas, good Bartholomew, we have trouble enough and more.

FATHER: We lead a miserable life.

BARTHOLOMEW: Dear me! But what is the matter?

MEG: We're so *crowded*.

JOSEPH: We don't have any room at all.

ALL: He's in my way. She won't give me any room. How can I work? (*Etc.*)

BARTHOLOMEW (*Raising hand for silence*): Say no more. By all the gray hairs in my long gray beard, you really do have a problem.

FATHER: Dear Bartholomew, you are the wisest man in all the village. Can't you think of some way to help us?

OTHERS: Yes, please help us. There must be some way. Help us.

BARTHOLOMEW (*Again raising hand for silence*): Perhaps I can help you. Tell me this, friend John—do you own any animals?

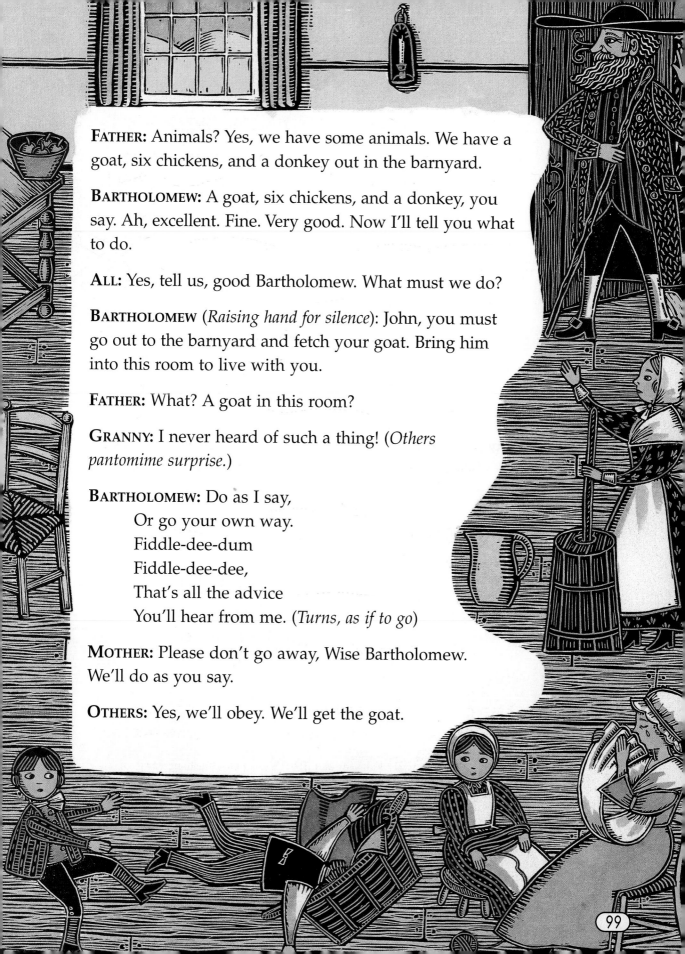

FATHER: Animals? Yes, we have some animals. We have a goat, six chickens, and a donkey out in the barnyard.

BARTHOLOMEW: A goat, six chickens, and a donkey, you say. Ah, excellent. Fine. Very good. Now I'll tell you what to do.

ALL: Yes, tell us, good Bartholomew. What must we do?

BARTHOLOMEW (*Raising hand for silence*): John, you must go out to the barnyard and fetch your goat. Bring him into this room to live with you.

FATHER: What? A goat in this room?

GRANNY: I never heard of such a thing! (*Others pantomime surprise.*)

BARTHOLOMEW: Do as I say,
      Or go your own way.
      Fiddle-dee-dum
      Fiddle-dee-dee,
      That's all the advice
      You'll hear from me. (*Turns, as if to go*)

MOTHER: Please don't go away, Wise Bartholomew. We'll do as you say.

OTHERS: Yes, we'll obey. We'll get the goat.

BARTHOLOMEW: Very well. In seven days and seven nights, I shall come again, to see how you are faring. Good day, my friends. (*Exits*)

FATHER: I suppose I'd better fetch the goat. (*Exits*)

MOTHER: A goat in this room!

JOAN: What a strange idea!

MEG (*Pulling her dolls close*): I'm scared of goats.

MARY ANN: Fiddlesticks! Old Bartholomew is the wisest man in the village. His advice *must* be good.

FATHER (*From offstage*): Watch out, everybody! Clear the way. Here comes the goat! (ALL *gather up their possessions, prepare to dodge, crying: "Ooooh! Watch out! The goat!" etc.* GOAT *rushes onstage, heading straight for* TOM *and* JOSEPH, *who run out of the* GOAT'S *path.* FATHER *tries to hold* GOAT *back by rope, but is pulled along instead.*)

ALL (*As* GOAT *charges around the stage*): Help! Watch out! He's coming this way! Help!

MOTHER (*Clutching head*): Oh, dear! Oh, dear!
  I very much fear
  That inviting this goat
  Was a bad idea!

       CURTAIN

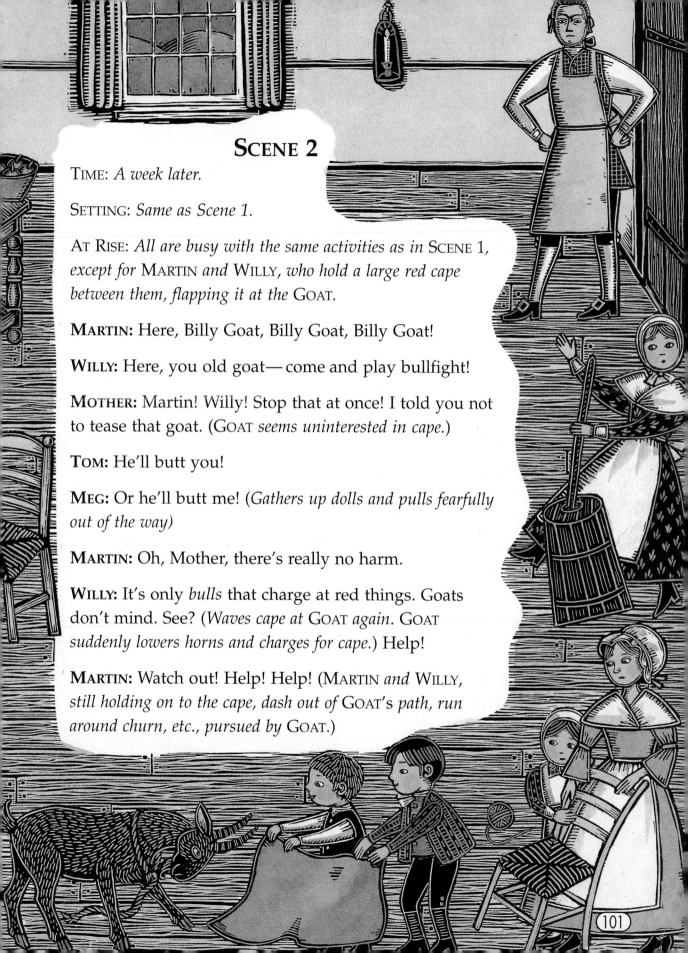

SCENE 2

TIME: *A week later.*

SETTING: *Same as Scene 1.*

AT RISE: *All are busy with the same activities as in* SCENE 1, *except for* MARTIN *and* WILLY, *who hold a large red cape between them, flapping it at the* GOAT.

MARTIN: Here, Billy Goat, Billy Goat, Billy Goat!

WILLY: Here, you old goat— come and play bullfight!

MOTHER: Martin! Willy! Stop that at once! I told you not to tease that goat. (GOAT *seems uninterested in cape.*)

TOM: He'll butt you!

MEG: Or he'll butt me! (*Gathers up dolls and pulls fearfully out of the way*)

MARTIN: Oh, Mother, there's really no harm.

WILLY: It's only *bulls* that charge at red things. Goats don't mind. See? (*Waves cape at* GOAT *again.* GOAT *suddenly lowers horns and charges for cape.*) Help!

MARTIN: Watch out! Help! Help! (MARTIN *and* WILLY, *still holding on to the cape, dash out of* GOAT's *path, run around churn, etc., pursued by* GOAT.)

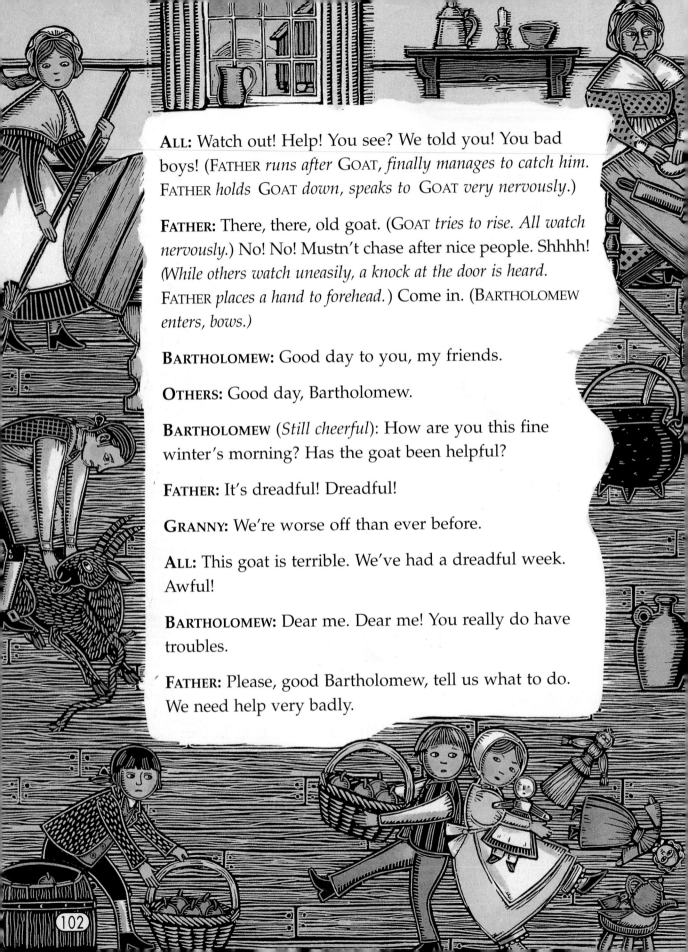

ALL: Watch out! Help! You see? We told you! You bad boys! (FATHER *runs after* GOAT, *finally manages to catch him.* FATHER *holds* GOAT *down, speaks to* GOAT *very nervously.*)

FATHER: There, there, old goat. (GOAT *tries to rise. All watch nervously.*) No! No! Mustn't chase after nice people. Shhhh! (*While others watch uneasily, a knock at the door is heard.* FATHER *places a hand to forehead.*) Come in. (BARTHOLOMEW *enters, bows.*)

BARTHOLOMEW: Good day to you, my friends.

OTHERS: Good day, Bartholomew.

BARTHOLOMEW (*Still cheerful*): How are you this fine winter's morning? Has the goat been helpful?

FATHER: It's dreadful! Dreadful!

GRANNY: We're worse off than ever before.

ALL: This goat is terrible. We've had a dreadful week. Awful!

BARTHOLOMEW: Dear me. Dear me! You really do have troubles.

FATHER: Please, good Bartholomew, tell us what to do. We need help very badly.

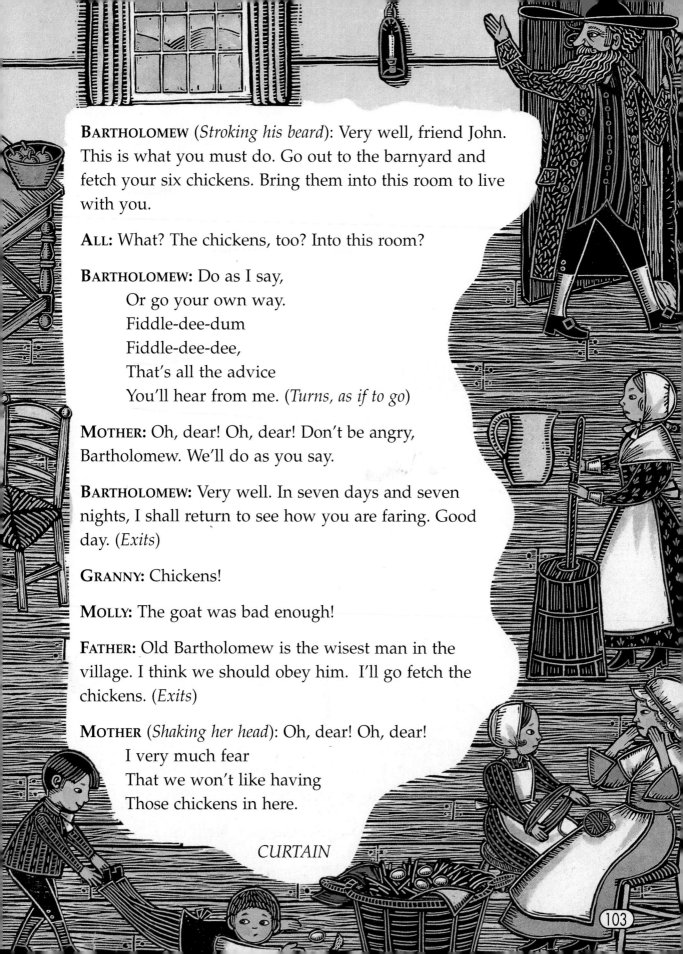

BARTHOLOMEW (*Stroking his beard*): Very well, friend John. This is what you must do. Go out to the barnyard and fetch your six chickens. Bring them into this room to live with you.

ALL: What? The chickens, too? Into this room?

BARTHOLOMEW: Do as I say,
　　Or go your own way.
　　Fiddle-dee-dum
　　Fiddle-dee-dee,
　　That's all the advice
　　You'll hear from me. (*Turns, as if to go*)

MOTHER: Oh, dear! Oh, dear! Don't be angry, Bartholomew. We'll do as you say.

BARTHOLOMEW: Very well. In seven days and seven nights, I shall return to see how you are faring. Good day. (*Exits*)

GRANNY: Chickens!

MOLLY: The goat was bad enough!

FATHER: Old Bartholomew is the wisest man in the village. I think we should obey him. I'll go fetch the chickens. (*Exits*)

MOTHER (*Shaking her head*): Oh, dear! Oh, dear!
　　I very much fear
　　That we won't like having
　　Those chickens in here.

CURTAIN

SCENE 3

TIME: *A week later.*

SETTING: *The same.*

AT RISE: *All are doing the same activities as before, but now they are more crowded than ever. The* GOAT *wanders around the stage, sniffing and butting everyone—and hopping, pecking, clucking everywhere are the* CHICKENS.

JOSEPH (*Shooing two* CHICKENS *away from his basket*): Shoo! Scat! (CHICKENS *squawk, flutter over to* MEG, *who shoos them away.*)

MARY ANN: Watch out for the goat!

MOTHER: Don't step on the chickens.

WILLY: Oh dear, I think I've stepped on an egg!

ALL (*Loudly, at once*): Shoo! Scat! Watch out! Keep that chicken away! Watch out for the goat! (*A knock is heard.*)

FATHER (*At the top of his lungs*): Quiet! (*Silence, except for* CHICKENS' *clucking*) I think I heard a knock. (*Knock is repeated.*) Come in.

BARTHOLOMEW (*Enters, bowing. Cheerily*): Good morrow to you, my friends. My, what lovely chickens!

MEG: They're not lovely—they're nasty!

ALL: They're awful! We're so crowded! We've had a terrible week! (CHICKENS *flutter about, clucking.*)

FATHER: Please, good Bartholomew. Help us.

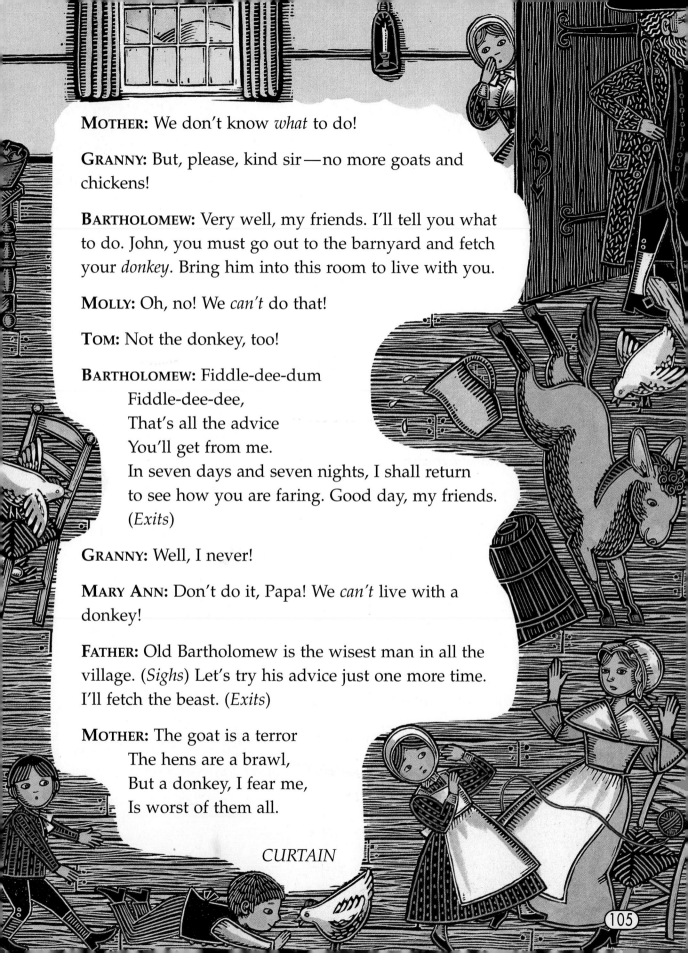

MOTHER: We don't know *what* to do!

GRANNY: But, please, kind sir—no more goats and chickens!

BARTHOLOMEW: Very well, my friends. I'll tell you what to do. John, you must go out to the barnyard and fetch your *donkey*. Bring him into this room to live with you.

MOLLY: Oh, no! We *can't* do that!

TOM: Not the donkey, too!

BARTHOLOMEW: Fiddle-dee-dum
　　　Fiddle-dee-dee,
　　　That's all the advice
　　　You'll get from me.
　　　In seven days and seven nights, I shall return
　　　to see how you are faring. Good day, my friends.
　　　(*Exits*)

GRANNY: Well, I never!

MARY ANN: Don't do it, Papa! We *can't* live with a donkey!

FATHER: Old Bartholomew is the wisest man in all the village. (*Sighs*) Let's try his advice just one more time. I'll fetch the beast. (*Exits*)

MOTHER: The goat is a terror
　　　The hens are a brawl,
　　　But a donkey, I fear me,
　　　Is worst of them all.

CURTAIN

SCENE 4

TIME: *A week later.*

SETTING: *The same.*

AT RISE: *All are doing the same activities as before, but with more difficulty than ever: The GOAT is butting everyone. The CHICKENS flutter, and squawk and peck. The DONKEY (two boys under a blanket) blunders around the stage, braying loudly.*

ALL: Shoo! Scat! Watch out for the goat! Don't step on the chickens! Here comes the donkey! Watch out! Help! Be careful!

FATHER: Oh, oh, oh! This is dreadful! I can't bear it another minute! (*A knock at the door is heard.*)

MEG: Papa, I think I heard someone knock.

GRANNY: If it's that Bartholomew again, I don't want to see him.

FATHER: Come in. (BARTHOLOMEW *enters, bowing as before. The family is silent, unfriendly. But the* DONKEY *brays, the* CHICKENS *cluck, and the* GOAT *baas.*)

BARTHOLOMEW: Good morrow to you, my friends. And how are the animals today?

MOTHER: The animals are fine, good sir, but we're *not!*

GRANNY (*Crossly, to* BARTHOLOMEW): Do you have any *more* good advice, kind sir?

BARTHOLOMEW (*Still cheerful. Stroking his beard*): Fiddle-dum, fiddle-dee; we'll see.

FATHER: Dear, good Bartholomew, you are still the wisest man in all the village. *Please* help us. We've never been so miserable.

BARTHOLOMEW (*Patting* DONKEY. *Looks up, as if astonished*): Do you mean to say that you don't *like* these nice animals?

JOAN (*Tartly*): Begging your pardon, sir, but you don't have to live with them.

BARTHOLOMEW: You don't like living with them?

ALL: NO!

BARTHOLOMEW (*Stroking his beard*): Well now, there's only one thing to do. John—

FATHER (*Fearfully*): Yes?

BARTHOLOMEW: Take all these animals—and put them back in the barnyard where they belong!

ALL: Hurray! (JOHN *and others chase all the animals offstage through the door; animals bray, cluck, and baa as they go off.*)

MOTHER: How wonderful! They're gone!

JOAN (*Puts broom aside. Stretches*): Mmmmm! Look at all this room we have now. I'm *so* glad they're gone!

MARTIN: I really think this room has grown bigger.

GRANNY: I never knew before how nice it was *not* to have a donkey in the room.

MARY ANN: Or a goat.

WILLY: Or chickens.

TOM: Come on, Meg. Spread your silly dollies out. There's plenty of room now. (*All turn happily to their tasks.*)

MOLLY: It's so quiet and peaceful.

FATHER: I'm so happy. I never knew how much room we had!

BARTHOLOMEW: Fiddle-dum, fiddle-dee,
    As I've said thrice before:
    I don't think you'll be needing
    My advice any more.
    Farewell, my friends. (*Walks toward exit, waving.*)

ALL (*Waving*): Farewell, good Bartholomew! Farewell! Thank you! (*Curtain*)

THE END

Think About It

1 How does Bartholomew help the family solve their problem?

2 What does the author of this play want you to learn?

3 Does this play take place in our time? How can you tell?

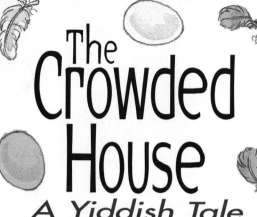

The Crowded House

A Yiddish Tale

retold by Pleasant deSpain
illustrated by Diane Paterson

Long ago there lived an unhappy man named Jacob. He lived in a tiny house with his wife, Leah, and their five children. The house was crowded!

The children played in every corner. Leah had little room for cooking and sewing. After a hard day of work in the fields, Jacob tried to rest by the fire in peace.

The house was noisy! The children yelled. Leah practiced her singing. Jacob couldn't hear himself think.

One day he went to the rabbi and asked for advice.

"I'm in a bad way," Jacob said. "My house is too small, and my family is too big.

The noise is making me crazy. What can I do?"

The rabbi thought and thought. Then he asked, "Do you have chickens in your front yard?"

"Yes," said Jacob. "We have seven chickens and one rooster."

"Move them into your house."

Jacob thought this strange, but he did as he was told.

A week later he returned to the rabbi, worse off than before.

"Help me, Rabbi. The chickens have taken over our house. They cluck and cluck and lay eggs in our beds. The rooster crows both day and night. My children can't sleep and Leah is upset. I'm so miserable."

The rabbi thought and thought. Then he asked, "Do you have a goat in the back yard?"

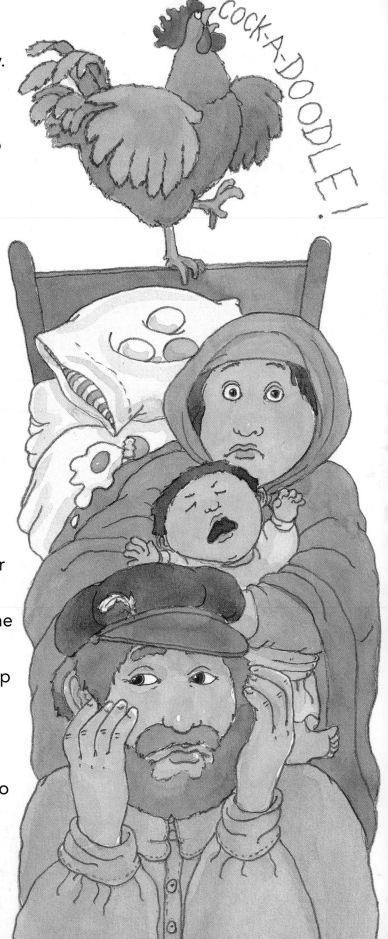

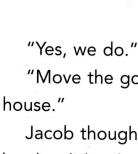

"Yes, we do."

"Move the goat into your house."

Jacob thought this strange, but he did as he was told.

A week later he returned to the rabbi.

"Please, please help me, Rabbi. The goat knocks us about, and chews our socks. The chickens fly up to the rafters and drop feathers in our soup. The children scream and cry. Leah is angry. I'm going crazy. What should I do?"

The rabbi thought and thought. Then he asked, "Do you have a cow in the field?"

"Yes," said Jacob.

"Move the cow into your house."

Jacob thought this strange, but he did as he was told.

He returned to the rabbi one week later. His head hung down.

"Oh Rabbi, my life is ruined. The cow takes up so much room. She moos and chews all day long. The goat bleats. The chickens cluck and the rooster crows. My children shout, and Leah is *so* mad at me. What can I do?"

The rabbi thought and thought. Then he said, "Take the chickens and the rooster out of your house. Take the goat out of your house. Take the cow out of your house."

Jacob ran home and did as he was told.

One week later he went to see the rabbi.

"You are such a wise man," he said. "My house has so much room! The children play quietly. Leah is happy. I didn't know how peaceful life could be. Thank you, dear Rabbi, thank you."

Think About It
How do you know the rabbi is wise?

113

RESPONSE ACTIVITIES

ACTION!

Pantomime a Scene

A pantomime is a kind of play in which the actors tell a story without words. With one or two classmates, choose a short scene from the play that you can act out without speaking. Perform your scene for other classmates.

ANOTHER SOLUTION

Write a Paragraph

Bartholomew helps the family learn an important lesson: *Be happy with what you have.* What if the family had asked *you* for advice? Think of another clever way to help them. Write a paragraph explaining your idea.

BE A PLAYWRIGHT

Write a Scene

"The Crowded House" is based on a folktale. Think of a folktale or fairy tale that you know well. Write a scene from it in the form of a play. Include stage directions in your scene.

MAKING CONNECTIONS

Compare and Contrast

"The Crowded House" and "The Crowded House: A Yiddish Tale" are different ways of retelling a folktale. Draw a chart to show how the play and the story are the same and how they are different. Think about the characters, the settings, and the ways the characters speak.

Wrap-Up

Share Your Story

COMPARE ORAL TRADITIONS
Some stories in this theme began as ways to explain things or to entertain people. Think about a story that you were told when you were younger. Share your story in a small group, and tell why you liked it. Then talk about how each person's story explains or entertains.

Tell Me Why

MAKE A CHART In this theme you read folktales, a fable, a tall tale, and a play. These stories were first told for different purposes — to teach or explain, to entertain, or to persuade. On a sheet of paper, make a chart like the one here to show the purpose of each selection.

Selection	Purpose
Coyote Places the Stars	
Why Mosquitoes Buzz in People's Ears	
The Ant and the Dove	
Cloudy With a Chance of Meatballs	

What's Your Opinion?

DO A SURVEY   Work with a small group of students to ask other classmates one of the following questions. Decide with your group how to graph what you learn.

- Which character would you like to be?
- Which selection did you like best?
- Which story's ending would you like to change?

Ask students who answer your question to give reasons for their answers. Tell some of the reasons when you present your graph to the class.

Which selection did you like best?	
Coyote Places the Stars	✓ ✓ ✓ ✓ ✓
Why Mosquitoes Buzz in People's Ears	✓ ✓ ✓
The Ant and the Dove	✓ ✓ ✓ ✓ ✓

THEME
GOOD

CONTENTS

NEIGHBORS

Cam Jansen and the
Triceratops Pops Mystery

by David A. Adler

MYSTERY

Using her amazing memory, Cam saves the day and solves another mystery.

Award-Winning Author

READER'S CHOICE LIBRARY

Mama Provi and
the Pot of Rice

by Sylvia Rosa-Casanova

REALISTIC FICTION

With the help of her neighbors, Mama Provi's pot of rice grows into a feast.

READER'S CHOICE LIBRARY

Choice

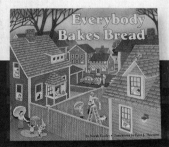

Fire! Fire!
by Gail Gibbons

NONFICTION

Firefighters are at work on land, in the sky, and on water.

Award-Winning Author and Illustrator

Farms Feed the World
by Lee Sullivan Hill

NONFICTION

Learn about the many reasons why farms are important to neighbors all over the world.

Everybody Bakes Bread
by Norah Dooley

REALISTIC FICTION

A rainy day gives Carrie a look at her neighbors' cooking (and a taste of it, too!).

Notable
Trade Book in
Social Studies

LEAH'S PONY

by Elizabeth Friedrich   Illustrated by Michael Garland

Leah's Pony

by Elizabeth Friedrich
illustrated by Michael Garland

The year the corn grew tall and straight, Leah's papa bought her a pony. The pony was strong and swift and sturdy, with just a snip of white at the end of his soft black nose. Papa taught Leah to place her new saddle right in the middle of his back and tighten the girth around his belly, just so.

That whole summer, Leah and her pony crossed through cloud-capped cornfields and chased cattle through the pasture.

Leah scratched that special spot under her pony's mane and brushed him till his coat glistened like satin.

Each day Leah loved to ride her pony into town just to hear Mr. B. shout from the door of his grocery store, "That's the finest pony in the whole county."

The year the corn grew no taller than a man's thumb, Leah's house became very quiet. Sometimes on those hot, dry nights, Leah heard Papa and Mama's hushed voices whispering in the kitchen. She couldn't understand the words but knew their sad sound.

Some days the wind blew so hard it turned the sky black with dust. It was hard for Leah to keep her pony's coat shining. It was hard for Mama to keep the house clean. It was hard for Papa to carry buckets of water for the sow and her piglets.

Soon Papa sold the pigs and even some of the cattle. "These are hard times," he told Leah with a puzzled look. "That's what these days are, all right, hard times."

Mama used flour sacks to make underwear for Leah. Mama threw dishwater on her drooping petunias to keep them growing. And, no matter what else happened, Mama always woke Leah on Saturday with the smell of fresh, hot coffee cake baking.

One hot, dry, dusty day grasshoppers turned the day to night. They ate the trees bare and left only twigs behind.

The next day the neighbors filled their truck with all they owned and stopped to say good-bye. "We're off to Oregon," they said. "It must be better there." Papa, Mama, and Leah waved as their neighbors wobbled down the road in an old truck overflowing with chairs and bedsprings and wire.

The hot, dry, dusty days kept coming. On a day you could almost taste the earth in the air, Papa said, "I have something to tell you, Leah, and I want you to be brave. I borrowed money from the bank. I bought seeds, but the seeds dried up and blew away. Nothing grew. I don't have any corn to sell. Now I can't pay back the bank," Papa paused. "They're going to have an auction, Leah. They're going to sell the cattle and the chickens and the pickup truck."

Leah stared at Papa. His voice grew husky and soft. "Worst of all, they're going to sell my tractor. I'll never be able to plant corn when she's gone. Without my tractor, we might even have to leave the farm. I told you, Leah, these are hard times."

Leah knew what an auction meant. She knew eager faces with strange voices would come to their farm. They would stand outside and offer money for Papa's best bull and Mama's prize rooster and Leah's favorite calf.

All week Leah worried and waited and wondered what to do. One morning she watched as a man in a big hat hammered a sign into the ground in front of her house.

Leah wanted to run away. She raced her pony past empty fields lined with dry gullies. She galloped past a house with rags stuffed in broken windowpanes. She sped right past Mr. B. sweeping the steps outside his store.

At last Leah knew what she had to do. She turned her pony around and rode back into town. She stopped in front of Mr. B.'s store. "You can buy my pony," she said.

Mr. B. stopped sweeping and stared at her. "Why would you want to sell him?" he asked. "That's the finest pony in the county."

Leah swallowed hard. "I've grown a lot this summer," she said. "I'm getting too big for him."

Sunburned soil crunched under Leah's feet as she walked home alone. The auction had begun. Neighbors, friends, strangers—everyone clustered around the man in the big hat. "How much for this wagon?" boomed the man. "Five dollars. Ten dollars. Sold for fifteen dollars to the man in the green shirt."

Papa's best bull.

Sold.

Mama's prize rooster.

Sold.

Leah's favorite calf.

Sold.

Leah clutched her money in her hand. "It has to be enough," she whispered to herself. "It just has to be."

"Here's one of the best items in this entire auction," yelled the man in the big hat. "Who'll start the bidding at five hundred dollars for this practically new, all-purpose Farmall tractor? It'll plow, plant, fertilize, and even cultivate for you."

It was time. Leah's voice shook. "One dollar."

The man in the big hat laughed. "That's a low starting bid if I ever heard one," he said. "Now let's hear some serious bids."

No one moved. No one said a word. No one even seemed to breathe.

"Ladies and gentlemen, this tractor is a beauty! I have a bid of only one dollar for it. One dollar for this practically new Farmall tractor! Do I hear any other bids?"

Again no one moved. No one said a word. No one even seemed to breathe.

"This is ridiculous!" the man's voice boomed out from under his hat into the silence. "Sold to the young lady for one dollar."

The crowd cheered. Papa's mouth hung open. Mama cried. Leah proudly walked up and handed one dollar to the auctioneer in the big hat.

"That young lady bought one fine tractor for one very low price," the man continued. "Now how much am I bid for this flock of healthy young chickens?"

"I'll give you ten cents," offered a farmer who lived down the road.

"Ten cents! Ten cents is mighty cheap for a whole flock of chickens," the man said. His face looked angry.

Again no one moved. No one said a word. No one even seemed to breathe.

"Sold for ten cents!"

The farmer picked up the cage filled with chickens and walked over to Mama. "These chickens are yours," he said.

The man pushed his big hat back on his head. "How much for this good Ford pickup truck?" he asked.

"Twenty-five cents," yelled a neighbor from town.

Again no one moved. No one said a word. No one
even seemed to breathe.

"Sold for twenty-five cents!" The man in the big
hat shook his head. "This isn't supposed to be a penny
auction!" he shouted.

The neighbor paid his twenty-five cents and took the
keys to the pickup truck. "I think these will start your
truck," he whispered as he dropped the keys into Papa's
shirt pocket.

Leah watched as friends and neighbors bid a penny for
a chicken or a nickel for a cow or a quarter for a plow. One
by one, they gave everything back to Mama and Papa.

The crowds left. The sign disappeared. Chickens
scratched in their coop, and cattle called for their corn.
The farm was quiet. Too quiet. No familiar whinny
greeted Leah when she entered the barn. Leah
swallowed hard and straightened her back.

That night in Leah's hushed house, no sad voices whispered in the kitchen. Only Leah lay awake, listening to the clock chime nine and even ten times. Leah's heart seemed to copy its slow, sad beat.

The next morning Leah forced open the heavy barn doors to start her chores. A loud whinny greeted her. Leah ran and hugged the familiar furry neck and kissed the white snip of a nose. "You're back!" she cried. "How did you get here?"

Then Leah saw the note with her name written in big letters:

Dear Leah,
*   This is the finest pony in the county. But he's a little bit small for me and a little bit big for my grandson.*
*   He fits you much better.*
*   Your friend,*
*   Mr. B.*
P.S. I heard how you saved your family's farm.
These hard times won't last forever.

And they didn't.

Think About It

1 How do Leah and her neighbors save the family's farm?

2 What is Mr. B. like? How do you know?

3 How do you think the people at the auction feel when Leah buys the tractor? Explain your answer.

Meet the Author

Readers can find out about new books by reading book reviews. A book review gives some information about the book, the author, and the illustrator. It also tells what the reviewer thinks of the book. This is what a book review might look like.

C-10 Friday, March 2

The Bigtown News

Leah's Pony a Delight

review by Maria Santos

"That's the best part about writing. It can take you anywhere!"

Leah's Pony is sure to please readers of all ages. The main character faces a choice between helping her family and keeping her pony. Children will understand how Leah feels about her difficult decision. Adults will find this warm, historical story interesting, too.

Author Elizabeth Friedrich loves to study history. She often wonders what it might have been like to live in another time. Her questions about the past led her to write this story about the Dust Bowl of the 1930s. "That's the best part about writing," she says. "It can take you anywhere!"

and the Illustrator
Elizabeth Friedrich
and Michael Garland

The Bigtown News

Friday, March 2 C-11

A picture book would not be complete without illustrations. The reader will find many beautiful paintings in *Leah's Pony.* Michael Garland did careful research to correctly show the cars, houses, and clothing of the 1930s. He even studied the work of Grant Wood, a well-known Midwestern artist of that time.

Garland used oil paints for the pictures in *Leah's Pony.* He is now creating some of his book art on a computer. "I'll still work in oils, but I'm eager to work on the computer," he says. He feels that the computer will make his work a little easier.

Together, Friedrich and Garland have created a book to remember!

"I'll still work in oils, but I'm eager to work on the computer."

**Visit *The Learning Site!*
www.harcourtschool.com**

Response

Thank You

WRITE A LETTER

Imagine that you are Leah or one of her parents. Write a letter to the other farmers, thanking them for their help. Be sure to tell them how you and your family are doing now.

Helpful Neighbors

LOOK FOR HELPERS

Leah's neighbors work together to save her family's farm. Find out about people in your community who help others. You might look for stories in the newspaper or on TV. You might also talk with family members or neighbors. If you can, interview a person who helps others. Share with your classmates what you learn.

Activities

Any Other Bids?

PERFORM A SKIT

With a group, act out the scene in which the auction takes place. You might like to use props in your skit, such as coins and keys. You could also use desks or chairs for the tractor and the pickup truck. Perform your skit for your classmates.

Family Farm Saved

WRITE A TV NEWS REPORT

The story of how Leah's farm was saved has made the evening news. You are the TV news reporter covering the story. Tell viewers how the community helped Leah's family keep their farm. Present your news report to your classmates.

Characters' Feelings and Action

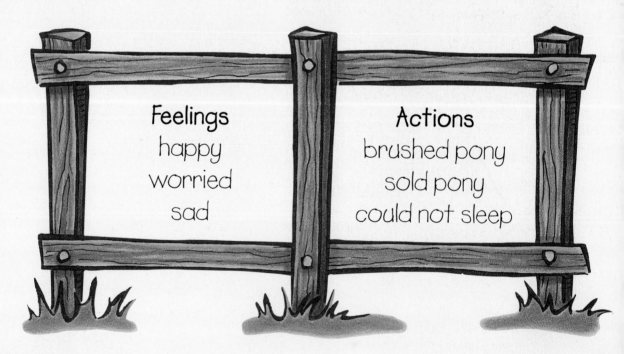

In the beginning of "Leah's Pony," Leah is happy. Later she is worried. You can tell how a character is feeling by noticing what the character says and does. You can also find clues in what the author and the other people in the story say about the character. What things does Leah do that help you understand how she is feeling during the story? What do the author and the other characters tell you about her?

A chart like the one below can help you think about characters' feelings and actions.

Feelings	Actions
happy	brushed pony
worried	sold pony
sad	could not sleep

When you read, it is important to understand the characters' feelings and actions. This helps you understand what kind of people they are. It can also make reading more interesting. In the story below, look for clues about how Maylee feels about her puppy.

When Maylee came home from school, she could not find her puppy. "I've lost Patches," she said, covering her face and crying. Suddenly a wet nose rubbed her leg. "Patches, you're back!" Maylee said, giving him a hug.

WHAT HAVE YOU LEARNED?

1 How can you tell what a character is feeling? How can understanding those feelings help you?

2 Imagine meeting Mr. B. What do you think he would be like? List words to describe him.

TRY THIS • TRY THIS • TRY THIS

Think of a character from a book or movie. Decide what this character is like by listing some of his or her feelings and actions.

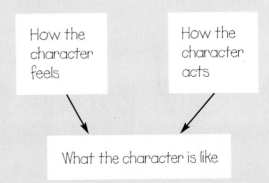

How the character feels

How the character acts

What the character is like

Visit *The Learning Site!* www.harcourtschool.com

The Three Little Javelinas

by Susan Lowell
illustrated by Jim Harris

Once upon a time, way out in the desert, there were three little javelinas. Javelinas (ha-ve-LEE-nas) are wild, hairy, southwestern cousins of pigs.

Their heads were hairy, their backs were hairy, and their bony legs—all the way down to their hard little hooves—were very hairy. But their snouts were soft and pink.

One day, the three little javelinas trotted away to seek their fortunes. In this hot, dry land, the sky was almost always blue. Steep purple mountains looked down on the desert, where the cactus forests grew.

Soon the little javelinas came to a spot where the path divided, and each one went a different way.

The first little javelina wandered lazily along. He didn't see a dust storm whirling across the desert—until it caught him.

The whirlwind blew away and left the first little javelina sitting in a heap of tumbleweeds. Brushing himself off, he said, "I'll build a house with them!" And in no time at all, he did.

Then along came a coyote. He ran through the desert so quickly and so quietly that he was almost invisible. In fact, this was only one of Coyote's many magical tricks. He laughed when he saw the tumbleweed house and smelled the javelina inside.

"Mmm! A tender juicy piggy!" he thought. Coyote was tired of eating mice and rabbits.

He called out sweetly, "Little pig, little pig, let me come in."

"Not by the hair of my chinny-chin-chin!" shouted the first javelina (who had a lot of hair on his chinny-chin-chin!).

"Then I'll huff, and I'll puff, and I'll blow your house in!" said Coyote.

And he huffed, and he puffed, and he blew the little tumbleweed house away.

But in all the hullabaloo, the first little javelina escaped—and went looking for his brother and sister.

Coyote, who was very sneaky, tiptoed along behind.

The second little javelina walked for miles among giant cactus plants called saguaros (sa-WA-ros). They held their ripe red fruit high in the sky. But they made almost no shade, and the little javelina grew hot.

Then he came upon a Native American woman who was gathering sticks from inside a dried-up cactus. She planned to use these long sticks, called saguaro ribs, to knock down the sweet cactus fruit.

The second little javelina said, "Please, may I have some sticks to build a house?"

"*Ha'u*," (ha-ou) she said, which means "yes" in the language of the Desert People.

When he was finished building his house, he lay down in the shade. Then his brother arrived, panting from the heat, and the second little javelina moved over and made a place for him.

Pretty soon, Coyote found the saguaro rib house. He used his magic to make his voice sound just like another javelina's.

"Little pig, little pig, let me come in!" he called.

But the little javelinas were suspicious. The second one cried, "No! Not by the hair of my chinny-chin-chin!"

"Bah!" thought Coyote. "I am not going to eat your *hair.*"

Then Coyote smiled, showing all his sharp teeth: "I'll huff, and I'll puff, and I'll blow your house in!"

So he huffed, and he puffed, and all the saguaro ribs came tumbling down.

But the two little javelinas escaped into the desert.

Still not discouraged, Coyote followed. Sometimes his magic did fail, but then he usually came up with another trick.

The third little javelina trotted through beautiful palo verde trees, with green trunks and yellow flowers. She saw a snake sliding by, smooth as oil. A hawk floated round and round above her. Then she came to a place where a man was making adobe (a-DOE-be) bricks from mud and straw. The bricks lay on the ground, baking in the hot sun.

The third little javelina thought for a moment, and said, "May I please have a few adobes to build a house?"

"Sí," answered the man, which means "yes" in Spanish, the brick-maker's language.

So the third javelina built herself a solid little adobe house, cool in summer and warm in winter. When her brothers found her, she welcomed them in and locked the door behind them.

Coyote followed their trail.

"Little pig, little pig, let me come in!" he called.

The three little javelinas looked out the window. This time Coyote pretended to be very old and weak, with no teeth and a sore paw. But they were not fooled.

"No! Not by the hair of my chinny-chin-chin," called back the third little javelina.

"Then I'll huff, and I'll puff, and I'll blow your house in!" said Coyote. He grinned, thinking of the wild pig dinner to come.

"Just try it!" shouted the third little javelina.

So Coyote huffed and puffed, but the adobe bricks did not budge.

Again, Coyote tried. "I'LL HUFF . . . AND I'LL PUFF . . . AND I'LL BLOW YOUR HOUSE IN!"

The three little javelinas covered their hairy ears.

But nothing happened. The javelinas peeked out the window.

The tip of Coyote's raggedy tail whisked right past their noses. He was climbing upon the tin roof. Next, Coyote used his magic to make himself very skinny.

"The stove pipe!" gasped the third little javelina. Quickly she lighted a fire inside her wood stove.

"What a feast it will be!" Coyote said to himself. He squeezed into the stove pipe. "I think I'll eat them with red hot chile sauce!"

Whoosh. S-s-sizzle!

Then the three little javelinas heard an amazing noise. It was not a bark. It was not a cackle. It was not a howl. It was not a scream. It was all of those sounds together.

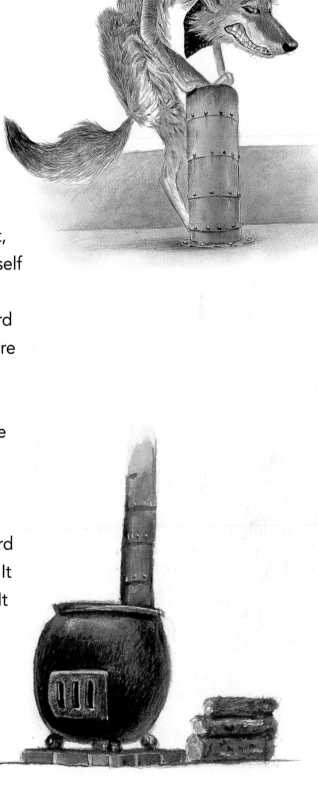

"Yip

     yap

        yeep

            YEE-OWW-OOOOOOOOOOOOOO!"

Away ran a puff of smoke shaped like a coyote.

The three little javelinas lived happily ever after in the adobe house.

And if you ever hear Coyote's voice, way out in the desert at night . . . well, you know what he's remembering!

Think About It

1 How do the javelinas depend on their community and on one another?

2 Compare this story to "The Three Little Pigs" or another story you know. How are the two stories alike? How are they different?

3 Which character do you like best? Explain why.

Postcards . . .
from the Author

Dear Readers,

Greetings from my home in the Sonoran Desert in Arizona! There are desert areas like this in parts of California, Texas, and New Mexico, too. I can see javelinas, coyotes, tumbleweeds, and cacti from my windows!

Much of the way of life in this part of the United States is based on Native American and Spanish cultures. The little javelinas' houses are like houses that have been built here for hundreds of years.

Why don't you write a story about where you live? Have fun!

Your friend,

Susan Lowell

Susan Lowell

from the Illustrator

Hi, Kids!

This is my home in Colorado, where I live on the north side of the Grand Mesa, the biggest flat-topped mountain in the world. This mesa is almost 11,000 feet high. From my windows I can look down into beautiful valleys.

My house is at the end of a dirt road. The stars seem to shine very brightly here because there aren't any other lights nearby.

Elk and deer wander onto my deck, and at night my family and I can sometimes hear coyotes howl. But guess what! No javelinas. They live in the Southwest.

Happy reading,

Jim Harris

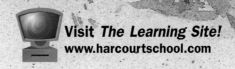

**Visit *The Learning Site!*
www.harcourtschool.com**

157

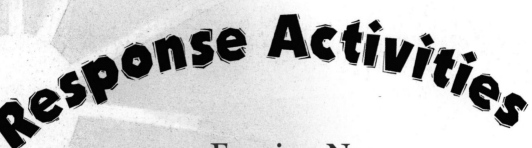

Response Activities

Evening News

INTERVIEW CHARACTERS

Imagine you are a television news reporter. You want to report on what happened to the coyote and the javelinas. Think of some questions to ask the characters in an interview. Ask some classmates to play the parts of characters from the story. Then perform your interview.

Adobe for Sale

WRITE A CLASSIFIED AD

The three little javelinas are moving and need to sell their home. Help them write an ad that will "grab" buyers' attention. Before you write your ad, read some real house-for-sale ads in the Classifieds section of a newspaper.

Tumbleweeds Needed

DRAW A DIAGRAM

Everywhere tumbleweeds roll, they
drop seeds that grow into new plants.
Some people who live in the Southwest
don't like tumbleweeds because there
are so many of them tumbling around.
Think of a clever way to use tumbleweeds
and keep them out of people's way.
Draw a diagram that shows your idea.

Pigs in Pittsburgh

WRITE A STORY

The author of this tale took a well-known
story and rewrote it with a new setting.
Write your own story about the
three little pigs with a new
setting. It might take place
in your neighborhood or in
another part of the world.
Draw some pictures to go
with your story.

159

By

DIANA APPELBAUM

Pictures by

HOLLY MEADE

COCOA

Chocolate comes from a faraway island where birds have pink feathers, leaves grow bigger than I am tall, and it is always summer. Children who live on the island never have to wear boots or clean ashes from the stove because winter never comes. Best of all on the island of always-summer, chocolate grows on trees.

The island where chocolate grows on trees is called Santo Domingo and I know all about it because Uncle Jacob sails there on a trading schooner. Once, he brought home a seashell for the mantel shelf. Inside, it is pink and smoother than anything in the world. If you hold it to your ear, it whispers, "Summer . . . summer . . . summer. . . ."

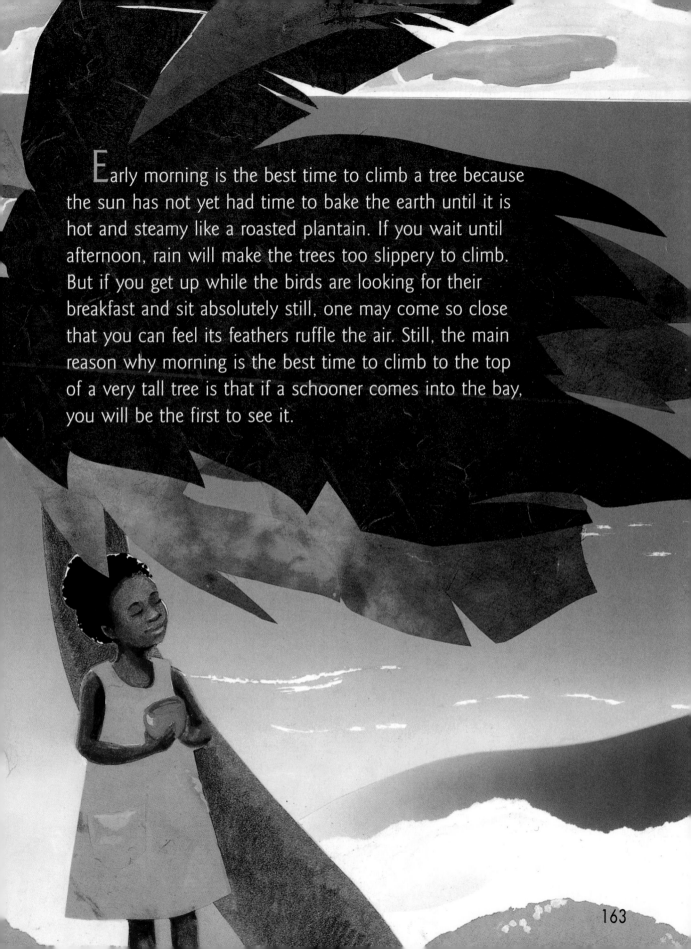

Early morning is the best time to climb a tree because the sun has not yet had time to bake the earth until it is hot and steamy like a roasted plantain. If you wait until afternoon, rain will make the trees too slippery to climb. But if you get up while the birds are looking for their breakfast and sit absolutely still, one may come so close that you can feel its feathers ruffle the air. Still, the main reason why morning is the best time to climb to the top of a very tall tree is that if a schooner comes into the bay, you will be the first to see it.

We have every kind of tree around our house: coconut, papaya, mango, orange, banana, plantain, breadfruit, guava, and a special kind called cacao—trees that grow chocolate. Cacao trees grow only in shade, so Papa plants young cacaos under tall banana trees that shade the growing cacao.

Little pink cacao flowers grow right on the trunk. Green cacao pods grow side by side with the flowers, and next to them grow ripe yellow and red pods, ready to be picked. A cacao tree is always blooming, always ripening, and always ready to harvest.

Papa splits the ripe cacao pods open with his machete and scoops out white pulp and pale beans. We spread slippery beans and sticky-sweet pulp on a carpet of banana leaves, then cover everything with more banana leaves.

I like to eat the sweet cacao pulp while we work, but I don't chew the beans! Once, I bit a fresh cocoa bean. It was so bitter it set my teeth on edge. Papa laughed and said, "Don't be so impatient, little one. Wait for the sun to make chocolate." And it does.

After a few hot days under the banana leaves, the pale, bitter cocoa beans begin to change color. We pick beans out of the old, smelly pulp and spread them to dry in the sun, turning them until they become a dark, beautiful brown.

Today the cocoa beans are drying. There is no work to do in the garden, and Papa says we are going conching. Mama wraps cassava bread in banana leaves and packs it in a basket with guavas for our lunch. It's hot paddling down the river San Juan, and we have a long way to go because after the river reaches the sea we must paddle along the beach until we reach a cove sheltered from ocean waves. I'm tired and thirsty when we finally pull the canoe onto the beach, so Papa opens coconuts and we drink their sweet milk. Now it is time to hunt for conchs.

I push my basket into the water and wade out until slippery leaves of turtle grass brush against my legs. Conchs are hiding in the turtle grass. Swimming slowly, I push the grass aside. Conchs look a lot like mossy rocks when they stand still, but I'll catch one if it hops.

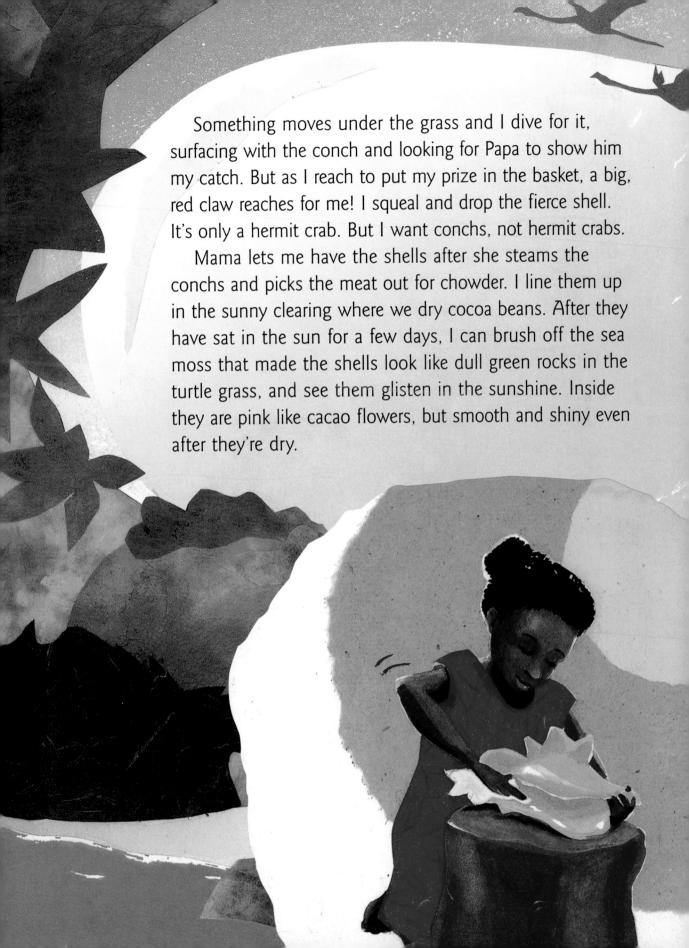

Something moves under the grass and I dive for it, surfacing with the conch and looking for Papa to show him my catch. But as I reach to put my prize in the basket, a big, red claw reaches for me! I squeal and drop the fierce shell. It's only a hermit crab. But I want conchs, not hermit crabs.

Mama lets me have the shells after she steams the conchs and picks the meat out for chowder. I line them up in the sunny clearing where we dry cocoa beans. After they have sat in the sun for a few days, I can brush off the sea moss that made the shells look like dull green rocks in the turtle grass, and see them glisten in the sunshine. Inside they are pink like cacao flowers, but smooth and shiny even after they're dry.

Our beans are not chocolate yet; they are only cocoa beans and we must turn them every day until they are dry. Mama roasts them over a hot fire until they begin to smell like chocolate. Then she lets me put them in the mortar and crush them. The best thing about being allowed to pound cocoa beans is the chocolate smell that curls up to your nose.

We put the crushed cocoa beans into a chocolate pot. While Mama boils the water, pours it over the beans, and adds sugar, I set out the cups. I think hot chocolate is the most wonderful drink in the whole world, unless there is an ice schooner in the bay.

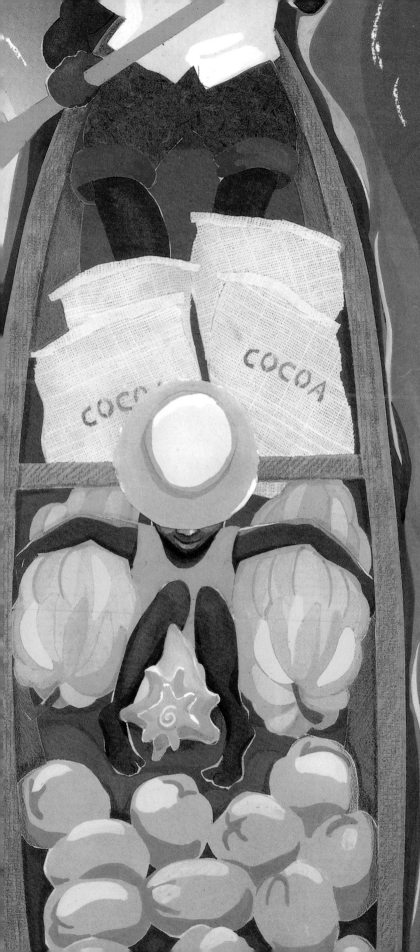

When a schooner comes, Papa drags his canoe to the river. It took a long time to hollow the canoe out of a log, and Papa is very careful never to drag it over a rock.

We pile the sacks of dried cocoa beans into the canoe, along with a heap of coconuts and bananas. I climb in between two bunches of bananas as big as I am, settle my best conch shell between my feet, and we're on our way.

Papa carries me up the side of the ship on a rope, and one of the sailors leans down to lift me over the rail. Other families have come and Papa must wait his turn to trade with the captain. Clutching my conch shell, I search the crowd for the sailor named Jacob who once showed me pictures of his faraway country. He spots me first, and says hello with a big smile.

I show Jacob my beautiful conch shell and let him feel how smooth and pink it is inside. He shows me a picture of a girl, just my age, with a ribbon in her hair. Then he pulls a small, square bag with stitching on it from his pocket. Jacob holds the bag to his face, sniffs it, and smiles. I sniff too. It doesn't smell like chocolate or jasmine or papaya or anything in the world. It smells strange and wonderful. And now it's mine.

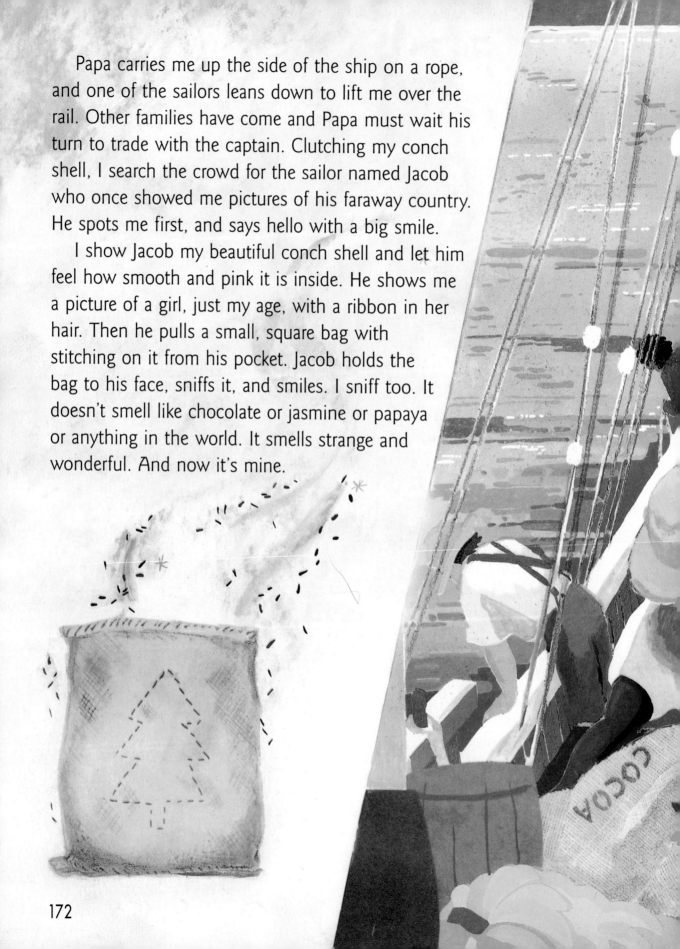

173

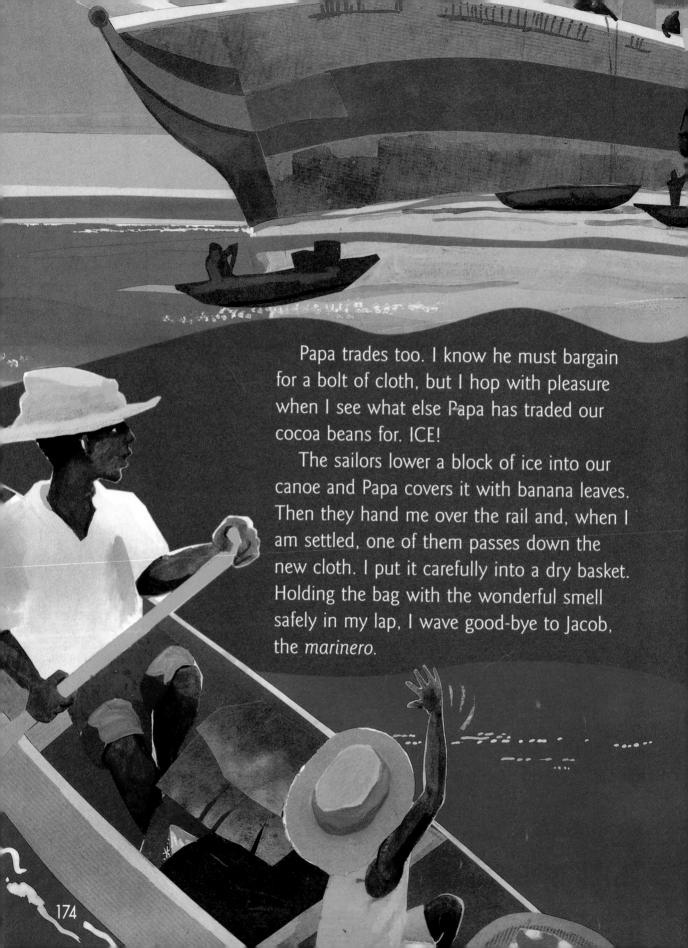

Papa trades too. I know he must bargain for a bolt of cloth, but I hop with pleasure when I see what else Papa has traded our cocoa beans for. ICE!

The sailors lower a block of ice into our canoe and Papa covers it with banana leaves. Then they hand me over the rail and, when I am settled, one of them passes down the new cloth. I put it carefully into a dry basket. Holding the bag with the wonderful smell safely in my lap, I wave good-bye to Jacob, the *marinero*.

When we get home, Mama scoops sweet, white pulp from a ripe cacao pod and beats it smooth and soft. Then she shaves the ice, stirs it into the cacao pulp, and pours it into cups for us to drink.

Cocoa ice is white and sweet and so cold I think it must be magic. It slides down my throat and makes me shiver to think of children living in such an icy place.

ICE

Ice schooners come from a land where the water is so hard that people walk on the river — right on the river. This place where water turns into ice is called Maine, and I know all about it because the sailor Jacob showed me pictures. In Maine the people build cooking fires inside their houses, and the trees don't have any leaves. And now I know another thing about Maine. I know that it has a wonderful smell. I sniff my balsam bag and try to imagine a land where children walk on rivers of ice.

Winter grips Maine hard. The days are short, bright, and so cold that sometimes nothing moves, not the wind, not the birds, not even the river.

177

But our kitchen is warm. Mama bakes apple pies in the big stove, and I practice my stitching by making a balsam pillow with fir needles. Papa and Uncle Jacob work for the ice company. If they can fill the big icehouses before spring breakup, Uncle Jacob's schooner and other ships can carry pieces of Maine winter to sell in hot countries far away. That's why we worry about snow.

Papa and Uncle Jacob and I stand on the riverbank stamping our boots, watching snow fall on new ice, and worrying.

"Figure it'll hold?" Papa asks, looking over the thin sheet of ice.

Uncle Jacob doesn't answer. They both know that air in the pockets of a million snowflakes will keep the river from freezing, and unless the river freezes there will be no ice to sell. But this ice is new and too thin to scrape. It has to be tapped—if it will hold the weight of a man.

We watch Uncle Jacob slide a wide plank onto the snowy surface and step out onto the river. It holds.

Soon a line of men follows Uncle Jacob. They inch forward, tapping holes in the ice with needle bars and mallets. River water seeps up through the holes, turning powder snow into a soggy slurry. If the weather stays cold, the icy water will freeze solid—thick enough to support a horse.

Horses are important once the ice is thick enough to scrape. After every snowstorm, Papa and Uncle Jacob harness our teams to heavy snow scrapers and clean snow off the river so the ice can freeze thick and clear. From Augusta all the way to Merrymeeting Bay, men and teams scrape snow to help the river freeze.

One morning when the sky is clear and there is no snow to scrape, Papa takes the wheels off the wagon box and puts the runners on. Mama bundles us in extra hats and mittens and tucks us into a pile of hay under a heavy quilt. Riding in a wagon on runners is like flying; we fly upriver clear to the falls! It's so cold that by morning the river has frozen more than a foot thick. Time to fill the icehouses.

I watch the ice boss rule a straight line across the river as though he were getting ready for a giant arithmetic lesson. Papa follows that line with the big ice cutter. The cutter's steel teeth slice through solid ice as easy as a knife slicing through Mama's apple pie, but Papa is careful not to cut through to the water. The ice has to stay solid enough to walk on until the whole surface has been grooved and cut into blocks. Back and forth they go, grooving and cutting until the river looks like a giant checkerboard, only—all the squares are white.

Fifty men are at work on the river today, grooving, cutting, sawing, and barring off blocks of ice, floating them across open water, pushing them into place on the elevator chain that lifts them toward the open door of the great icehouse. The upper doors are higher than the roof of the church, and the ice boss aims to fill it to the rafters before breakup.

I watch until I get so cold I have to run into the kitchen. Mama makes hot chocolate to warm me up.

Ice isn't worth anything unless you can get it all the way to summer without melting. That's why icehouse walls are built double, two walls with a wide space between, filled with sawdust to keep the cold in. That's why even icehouse doors are built double and filled with sawdust to keep summer out. And why we insulate the ice with a blanket of sweet meadow hay. When Uncle Jacob cuts the bales open, the green smell of summer meadows spills from the hay and fills the loft.

The men fill the great building one room at a time, lining blocks of ice up in perfect rows. Straight lines of ice that reach from wall to wall and rise in towers until they almost touch the roof. After the icehouse is full, the boss closes the doors and waits for the river to break up.

No matter how cold winter is, summer always comes. New grass in the pasture feels soft on my toes, and schooners come back up the Kennebec. Sailors fill the holds with ice, pouring a thick layer of sawdust all around as they stack it, and covering the sawdust with hay from our meadows.

Mama says ice from our river goes halfway around the world in ships that come home filled with silk and cashmere, ginger and tea. But the most important ship of all is the ice schooner Uncle Jacob is sailing on today, bound for Santo Domingo to bring home chocolate.

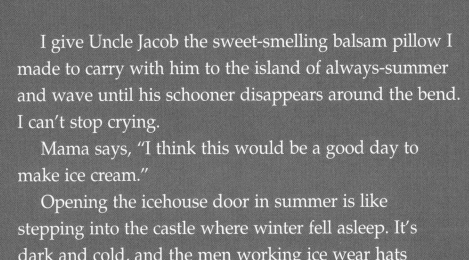

I give Uncle Jacob the sweet-smelling balsam pillow I made to carry with him to the island of always-summer and wave until his schooner disappears around the bend. I can't stop crying.

Mama says, "I think this would be a good day to make ice cream."

Opening the icehouse door in summer is like stepping into the castle where winter fell asleep. It's dark and cold, and the men working ice wear hats and gloves and woolen leggings even on the hottest summer day. They're busy moving ice into the holds of ships lined up at the wharf, but not too busy to set a frozen chunk of winter into the back of our wagon.

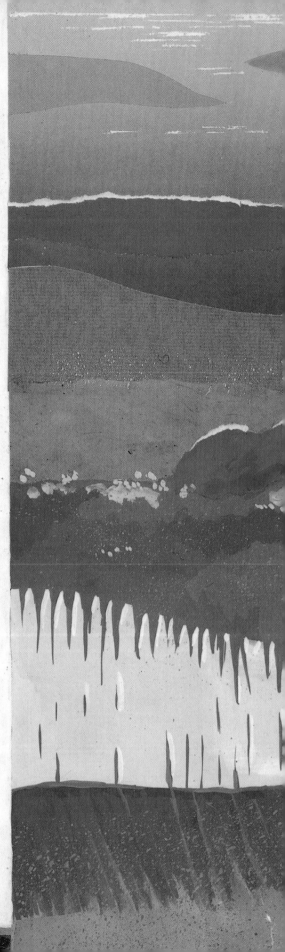

Mama measures cream and sugar into the can of the ice cream freezer while I carefully pour in the cocoa. Papa chips the ice and packs it around the can with layers of salt. Then I start to turn the crank. It turns easily at first, gentle strokes swirling chocolate, cream, and sugar round and round the dasher. But as the cream begins to freeze, my arm grows tired and the crank turns slow and slower until I can't turn it at all. Then Mama takes over and cranks until the ice cream is so hard the dasher won't turn another inch. When that happens, Mama sets the can on ice to keep until dinner and gives me the dasher to lick.

As I sit on the kitchen step licking chocolate from the ice-cold dasher, I close my eyes and imagine the island of always-summer, where giant pink seashells line the beaches and children pick chocolate from trees.

Think About It

1. How does the trading of goods help the people in this story?

2. Why is the character Uncle Jacob important?

3. In which of the two communities would you prefer to live? Why?

Meet the Author
Diana Appelbaum

Diana Appelbaum lives in New England, where she studies and writes about history. As a child, Diana loved to read about real people. She enjoyed stories that told what life was like long ago for people all over the world.

Diana Appelbaum is now a historian. She does a lot of research about the past. Through her books, she shares with others the interesting things she learns. Diana Appelbaum feels that history is very important. "You can't understand the present unless you know about the past," she says.

Visit *The Learning Site!*
www.harcourtschool.com

Meet the Illustrator
Holly Meade

Holly Meade has been illustrating children's books since 1991. Before that, she worked as an artist for a magazine and a flag company. In 1997, the American Library Association awarded Holly Meade a Caldecott Honor for illustrating *Hush! A Thai Lullaby*. This award is given to illustrators of American picture books for children.

Holly Meade uses gouache, or watercolor paints, and cut or torn paper to create her artwork. Just as authors rewrite their stories, artists often have to change their illustrations several times. Holly Meade says that she makes hundreds of drawings for each picture book she illustrates.

"Working on *Cocoa Ice* was exciting," says Holly Meade. She found it a challenge to illustrate both a warm, tropical place and a cold, wintry place in the same book.

Holly Meade

RESPONSE ACTIVITIES

So Far, So Near

WRITE A PARAGRAPH

Trade, or buying and selling, helps bring the people from Maine and Santo Domingo together. Write a paragraph. Tell how the two communities in the story help each other, even though they are so far apart.

Greetings from Far Away

DESIGN POSTCARDS

Make two postcards, one from Santo Domingo and one from Maine. On one side of each postcard, draw a picture of the place. On the other side, make spaces for a message and an address. You might send your postcards to a friend.

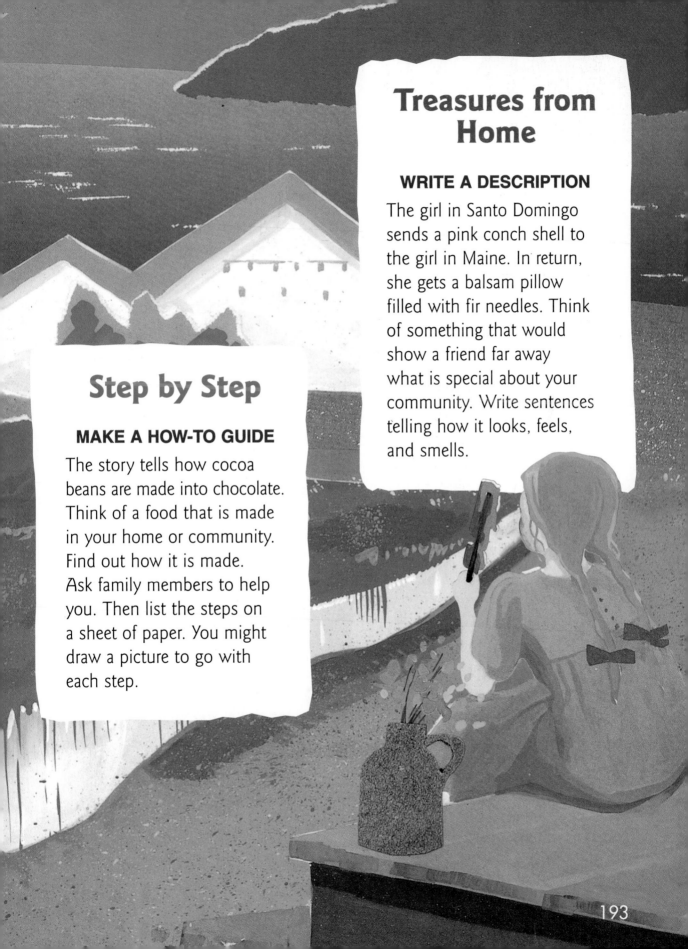

Treasures from Home

WRITE A DESCRIPTION

The girl in Santo Domingo sends a pink conch shell to the girl in Maine. In return, she gets a balsam pillow filled with fir needles. Think of something that would show a friend far away what is special about your community. Write sentences telling how it looks, feels, and smells.

Step by Step

MAKE A HOW-TO GUIDE

The story tells how cocoa beans are made into chocolate. Think of a food that is made in your home or community. Find out how it is made. Ask family members to help you. Then list the steps on a sheet of paper. You might draw a picture to go with each step.

"Cocoa Ice" is a story that gives a lot of information. How could you tell this story in just one or two sentences? First, you would need to decide what parts of "Cocoa Ice" are the most important.

When you use your own words to tell the most important events in a story, you are **summarizing** the story. Read the chart below to learn more about summarizing.

What Is a Good Summary?

IT SHOULD	IT SHOULD NOT
• tell about the most important ideas or the main things that happened	• tell about things that are not important
• follow the same order as the story	• tell about things that are not in the story
• be much shorter than the story	

Read the two sentences about "Cocoa Ice" below. Which sentence is a good summary?

People do not have to trade ice any more because we have freezers.

One family makes cocoa, another family makes ice, and they trade.

WHAT HAVE YOU LEARNED?

1. What does a good summary include?

2. Think about a science lesson. Imagine that one of your classmates was absent. Summarize the lesson for your classmate.

TRY THIS • TRY THIS • TRY THIS

Look in a children's encyclopedia to find out more about Maine or Santo Domingo. What is the most important information you read? Use the information to write a summary of the article.

Visit *The Learning Site!*
www.harcourtschool.com

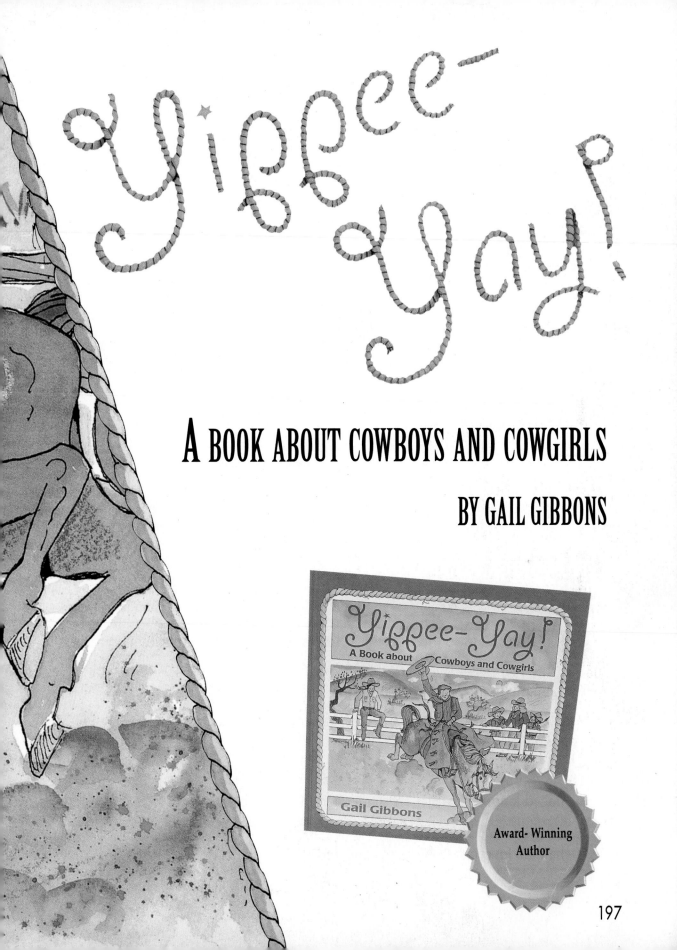

Yippee-Yay!

A BOOK ABOUT COWBOYS AND COWGIRLS

BY GAIL GIBBONS

Award-Winning Author

COWGIRL

COWBOY

From the 1860s to the 1890s, the Old West was a rough and wild frontier. It was the era of the American cowboy. Not many women lived in the Old West, and there were only a few cowgirls. Besides, at that time, the work of a cowboy was considered too harsh for most women.

Wealthy ranchers owned large tracts of land on which they grazed longhorn cattle. These ranchers hired cowboys, whose lives centered around tending the cattle, rounding them up, and moving them on long cattle drives for sale and profit.

A cowboy's clothing was chosen for rough wear and tear. Many cowboys wore the same clothes for months at a time. Some even slept in them! Smelly and caked in dirt, these clothes were often burned after a long cattle drive.

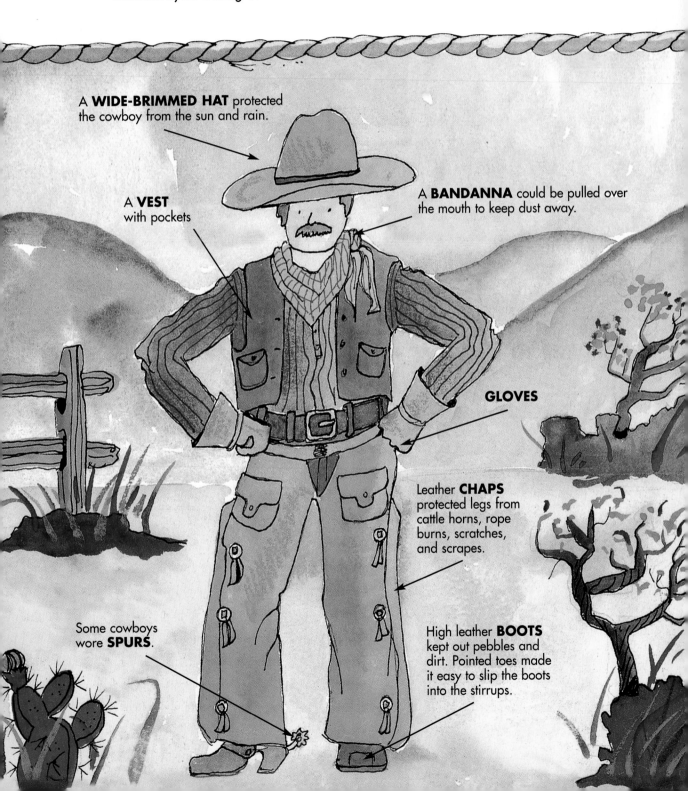

A **WIDE-BRIMMED HAT** protected the cowboy from the sun and rain.

A **VEST** with pockets

A **BANDANNA** could be pulled over the mouth to keep dust away.

GLOVES

Leather **CHAPS** protected legs from cattle horns, rope burns, scratches, and scrapes.

Some cowboys wore **SPURS**.

High leather **BOOTS** kept out pebbles and dirt. Pointed toes made it easy to slip the boots into the stirrups.

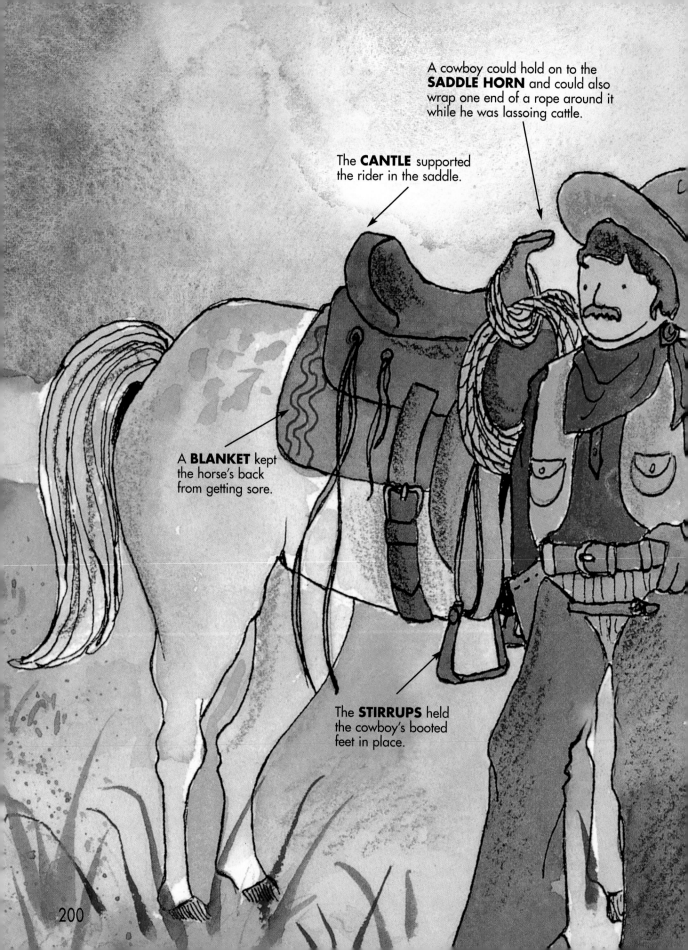

A cowboy could hold on to the **SADDLE HORN** and could also wrap one end of a rope around it while he was lassoing cattle.

The **CANTLE** supported the rider in the saddle.

A **BLANKET** kept the horse's back from getting sore.

The **STIRRUPS** held the cowboy's booted feet in place.

The **BRIDLE** controlled and guided the horse.

A cowboy's prized possession was his saddle. Without one, a cowboy couldn't work. The saddle had to be comfortable. Cowboys spent much of their time riding horses and ponies owned by the ranchers. Often the horse or pony became a cowboy's best partner.

Roping was the most difficult skill for a cowboy to learn, and it was the most important. Cowboys carried ropes called lariats to lasso cattle. It took many months of practice to learn to spin the lariat and release it at just the right moment.

LARIAT

A **BRONCO** is a partially tamed horse or pony that bucks.

BRONCOBUSTER

BUCKAROOS were assistants.

A **CORRAL** is a fenced-in area.

Wild horses had to be captured and tamed before they could work among the cattle. A skilled cowboy called a broncobuster would mount and ride the wild horse until it would trot obediently around the corral. What a wild ride! Busting, or breaking, horses was a very dangerous job.

Ranchers were unable to fence in the entire boundary of their many acres of land. So longhorns from different ranches would graze together freely. Once or twice a year, ranches held roundups. All the cattle and newborn calves would be rounded up, or brought to one location.

It was hard work to round up all those critters. Cattle are wild and fast. Any longhorn trying to get away would be lassoed and captured. The cowboy had a loop at the end of his lariat. When he twirled it and let it fly, the rope would snag the animal from afar. No cowboy wanted to get too close to an angry longhorn!

When the cattle were finally rounded up, the trail boss from each camp would count his herd. He could tell which longhorns belonged to his ranch by a mark on his cattle, called a brand. The calves didn't have brands. They were easy to identify because they followed their mothers.

Next, the cowboys lassoed the calves. This was called chopping out. One by one, the calves were brought to a wood fire filled with heated branding irons. The cowboys took turns pressing a branding iron to each calf's hip, leaving a mark.

Any stray steer within their own herd was lassoed, identified by its brand, and returned to the correct ranch. This was called cutting out.

Some common brands were

The Lazy J

The Flying V

The Scissors

The Quarter Circle T

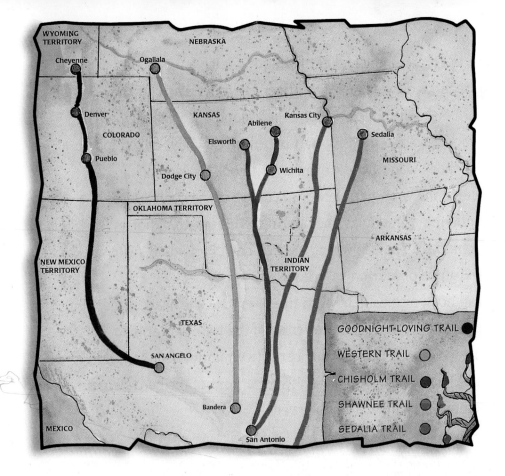

Cowboys who stole cattle from other ranches were called rustlers. These outlaws used a running iron to change the captured animals' brands to match their own. Pictures of rustlers' faces often appeared on wanted posters, and big rewards were promised for their arrest.

After the roundup came the trail drive. The best and the biggest longhorns would be moved in one huge herd along a trail to the closest town with a railroad station, called a railhead. The cattle were then brought to market by train.

Some trails were very long, nearly a thousand miles. Cowboys could drive the herd for only about ten to fifteen miles a day. They didn't want to push the cattle too hard, or they would lose weight, and they also took time to stop and let the animals graze along the way. Cattle drives could take many months. Only the toughest cowboys went on them.

A herd of several thousand cattle might stretch a mile along the trail and be tended by as many as fifteen cowboys. Each cowboy had his own task. The chuck wagon rolled along ahead of the herd, carrying food, cooking utensils, and bedding. Cowboys called food chuck. The chuck wagon was driven by the cook, called cookie.

Next came the wrangler. He was in charge of the spare horses, often numbering as many as one hundred. This group of horses was called a *remuda*, a Spanish word. The trail cowboys would switch to fresh horses three or four times a day.

The trail boss, also called the foreman, rode at the head of the herd. This cowboy had good knowledge of the trail, was able to communicate with the Native Americans they might encounter, and was an excellent tracker. As the cattle in the front of the herd began to move along, the other cattle followed.

REMUDA

WRANGLER

TRAIL BOSS
Also called the **FOREMAN**

POINT RIDER

The front of the herd was called the point position. The most experienced cowboys rode as point riders. They guided the steer in an arrowhead shape, keeping the pace and moving them along in the right direction. Cowboys called swing riders moved the herd forward and made sure the cattle didn't spread out too far.

The flank riders kept the cattle within the herd, preventing strays. The rear of the herd was called the drag position. The drag cowboys had the worst job of all. They rode through thick clouds of dust, urging slowpokes along and keeping an eye out for rustlers.

Some days the cowboys were in the saddle for sixteen hours—
a long, hard day. Because the cookie traveled ahead with the chuck
wagon, he was able to have food cooked and ready when the trail
team arrived. A meal was usually pork and beans, sourdough bread,
and coffee. "Come and get it!" he would call.

The cowboys often joked with the cookie while they ate their meal.

Many nights, cowboys would sit around the campfire, telling
stories and singing old cowboy songs. It was a time to relax and
gaze up at the never-ending sky filled with twinkling stars. Some
cowhands used their saddles as pillows when they settled down in
their bedrolls to sleep.

Day after day, the cattle moved along the dusty trail. What the
cowboys feared most was a stampede. Cattle were easily spooked.

Oh, give me a home where the buffalo roam,
Where the deer and the antelope play,
Where seldom is heard a discouraging word,
And the skies are not cloudy all day.

Home, home on the range,
Where the deer and the antelope play,
Where seldom is heard a discouraging word,
And the skies are not cloudy all day.

Thunder and lightning or any strange noise could send the herd charging in a panic. It was the cowboys' job to get the herd back under control. Many cowboys were injured or killed carrying out this task.

After a long, hard journey, the cowboys and cattle at last made their way into town. The cowboys moved the cattle into pens near the railroad tracks. From there, the cattle would travel by train to points east. The rancher was paid for the steer, and the cowboys were paid for their work. It was time to have fun!

The first thing a cowboy wanted to do was soak in a hot tub. What a treat to get a haircut and a shave and to buy new clothes! The cowboys would then sing, dance, and have fun on the town. The sheriff always stayed nearby to be sure that law and order prevailed.

Back then, cowboys and cowgirls showed off their skills at rodeos—and they still do today. The word *rodeo* comes from the Spanish word *rodear,* meaning to encircle or round up. People in the stands cheer as cowboys and cowgirls compete for prizes.

Rodeos feature five main events: bronco riding, bull riding, bareback riding, steer wrestling, and calf roping. It's a colorful and rowdy scene!

Today, cowboys and cowgirls still tend cattle and have roundups. But the days of the long cattle drives are over. Railroads can now be found near almost every cattle ranch. Many cowhands have college degrees in agriculture and livestock breeding.

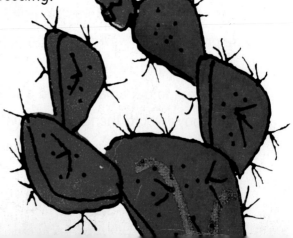

Cowhands drive pickup trucks and tractors and sometimes fly airplanes or helicopters to spot stray cattle. Cowboys and cowgirls today are still skilled in roping, branding, and riding horseback, just like the cowboys and cowgirls of the Old West.

Think About It

1. How is a cowboy's life different today from what it was in the past?

2. Is this selection fact or fiction? How can you tell?

3. What parts of being a cowboy or cowgirl would you like and dislike the most? Explain why.

211

More Facts About Cowboys and Cowgirls

The best-known cowboy hat is the Stetson, called the John B. after its maker, John B. Stetson.

Cowboys in South America are called gauchos. In Chile, they are called *huasos,* and in England, drovers.

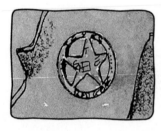

The Texas Rangers were formed in 1835 to deal with outlaws, cattle rustlers, and conflicts with Native Americans.

The trail boss sometimes paid a toll to Native Americans when crossing their land. They paid as much as ten cents per steer or gave a few longhorns in trade.

Between the 1860s and the 1890s, there were about forty thousand working cowboys and cowgirls.

The American cowboy has always been a symbol of freedom and bravery.

Meet the Author and Illustrator
Gail Gibbons

Gail Gibbons has written more than sixty nonfiction books for children. We asked her about writing *Yippee-Yay!*

QUESTION: How did you become interested in learning about cowboys?

GAIL GIBBONS: A few years ago, I was at the Sonora Desert Museum in Arizona, doing research for another book. While I was there, I took a few side trips to some cattle ranches. I asked some librarian friends if there were any simple nonfiction books about cowboys and cowgirls. They said it would be wonderful if I wrote one.

QUESTION: What kind of research did you do for *Yippee-Yay!*?

GIBBONS: I talked to people at rodeos and people who run ranches. I also went to Tombstone, Arizona, to get the feeling of what a western town might have been like back in the Wild West days.

QUESTION: What is the most interesting fact about cowboys and cowgirls that you discovered in your research?

GIBBONS: The most interesting fact I learned was that on cattle drives each cowboy had a specific job to do. Cattle drives required team effort!

Visit *The Learning Site!*
www.harcourtschool.com

WORK

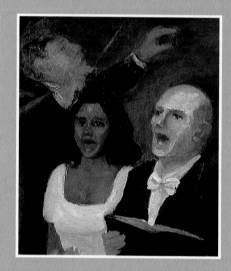

SONG

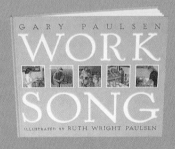

WRITTEN BY
GARY PAULSEN

ILLUSTRATED BY
RUTH WRIGHT
PAULSEN

Award-Winning
Author

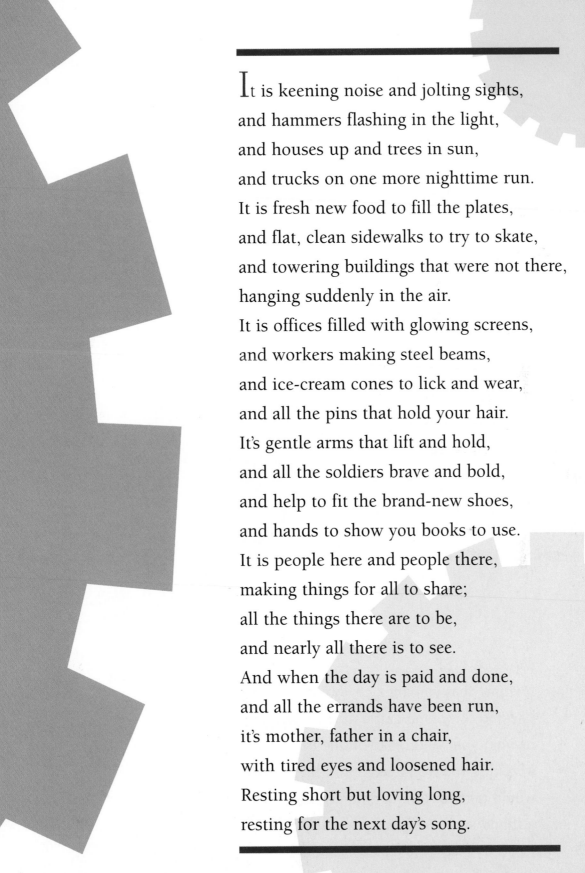

It is keening noise and jolting sights,
and hammers flashing in the light,
and houses up and trees in sun,
and trucks on one more nighttime run.
It is fresh new food to fill the plates,
and flat, clean sidewalks to try to skate,
and towering buildings that were not there,
hanging suddenly in the air.
It is offices filled with glowing screens,
and workers making steel beams,
and ice-cream cones to lick and wear,
and all the pins that hold your hair.
It's gentle arms that lift and hold,
and all the soldiers brave and bold,
and help to fit the brand-new shoes,
and hands to show you books to use.
It is people here and people there,
making things for all to share;
all the things there are to be,
and nearly all there is to see.
And when the day is paid and done,
and all the errands have been run,
it's mother, father in a chair,
with tired eyes and loosened hair.
Resting short but loving long,
resting for the next day's song.

Response

Making Connections

CREATE A JOB POSTER

The people in "Yippee-Yay!" and "Worksong" all have jobs to do. Look up information about some of the jobs that people in your community do. Find out how these jobs help your community. Make a poster about some of these important jobs.

Yee-Haw!

MAKE A LIST

Imagine that you are a cowboy or cowgirl packing for a long cattle drive. Make a list of what you would take on the trip. Think of things you would need and things you would take for fun. Compare your list with a friend's list. Did you forget anything?

Activities

Famous Cowhands

WRITE A REPORT

Use encyclopedias, books about the Old West, or the Internet to look up information about a famous cowboy or cowgirl. Find out when and where this cowhand lived and what he or she is known for. Then write a short report about the person.

Wrangler for Hire

ROLE-PLAY

Imagine that you are trying to get a job as a cowboy or cowgirl. Have a partner play the part of the trail boss. Tell the trail boss what job you are interested in. Do you want to be a wrangler, a point rider, or a swing rider? Then tell the trail boss why you think you would be good for the job.

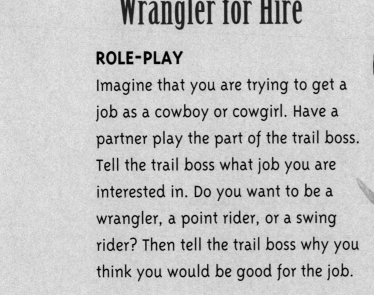

The sign reads:

CHEERFUL AND WILLING
HELPERS
WANTED
by MARVELOSISSIMO
THE MATHEMATICAL MAGICIAN

If You Made a MILLION

by David M. Schwartz

pictures by Steven Kellogg

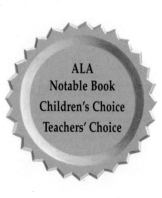

ALA
Notable Book
Children's Choice
Teachers' Choice

CONGRATULATIONS!
YOU'VE EARNED A PENNY.

It will buy anything that costs one cent.

WELL DONE!
YOU'VE MADE A NICKEL.

ONE NICKEL

is worth the same as FIVE PENNIES

HOORAY!
NOW YOU HAVE A DIME.

ONE DIME

has the same value as TWO NICKELS

or TEN PENNIES

220

EXCELLENT!
FOR YOUR HARD WORK YOU'VE EARNED A QUARTER.

ONE QUARTER

is the same amount of money as FIVE NICKELS

or TWO DIMES AND ONE NICKEL

or THREE NICKELS AND ONE DIME

or TWENTY-FIVE PENNIES

BLOW UP this BOA Earn 25¢

WONDERFUL!
YOU ARE NOW A DOLLAR RICHER.

ONE DOLLAR

is worth as much as FOUR QUARTERS

FIX THIS
FOUNTAIN'S FLOW

Earn $1.

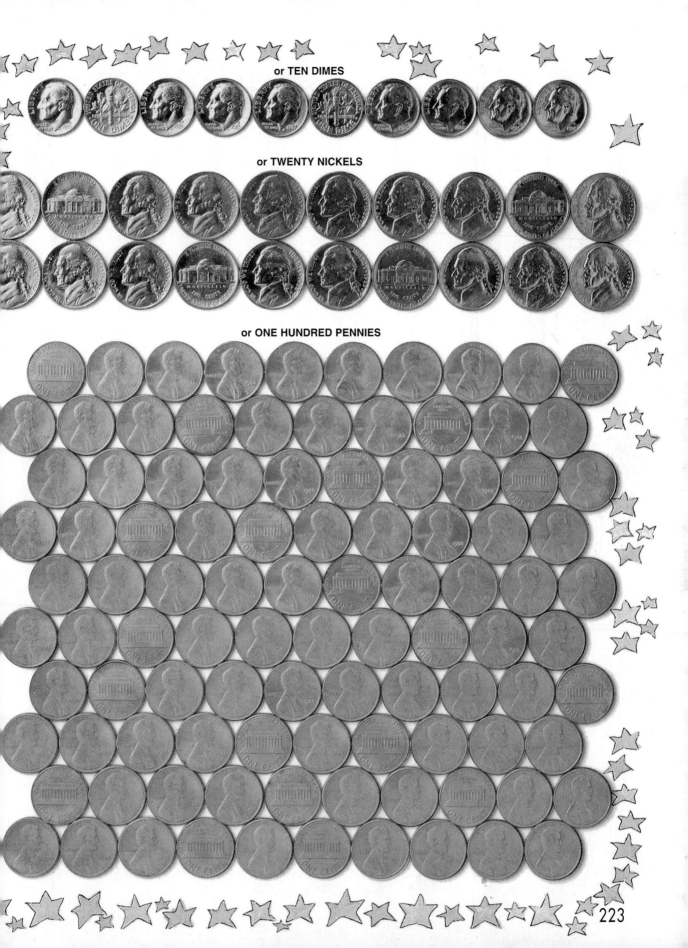

or TEN DIMES

or TWENTY NICKELS

or ONE HUNDRED PENNIES

223

You could use your dollar to buy one hundred
pieces of penny candy, or twenty five-cent balloons,

or ten stickers for ten cents each, or four rubber balls that cost twenty-five cents apiece.

Or perhaps you'd like to save your dollar. You could put it in the bank, and a year from now it will be worth $1.05.

The bank wants to use your money, and it will pay you five cents to leave your dollar there for a year. The extra five cents is called interest.

If you waited ten years, your dollar would earn
sixty-four cents in interest just from sitting in the bank.

Are you interested in earning lots of interest?
Wait twenty years, and one dollar will grow to $2.70.

DELICIOUS!
YOU'VE BAKED A CAKE AND EARNED FIVE DOLLARS.

You could be paid with one five-dollar bill or five
one-dollar bills. It doesn't matter. They have the same value.

STUPENDOUS!
YOU'VE MADE TEN DOLLARS.

How would you like to be paid? One ten-dollar bill? Two
five-dollar bills? Ten one-dollar bills? Or perhaps one five
and five ones? Take your pick—they're all worth ten dollars.

If you prefer coins, you can have a five-foot stack of pennies (that's one thousand of them) or a fifteen-inch stack of two hundred nickels. You could also be paid with one hundred dimes, which would stack up to just over five inches. Or you can receive your ten dollars as a $3\frac{1}{4}$-inch pile of forty quarters.

You could spend your ten dollars on ten kittens or one thousand kitty snacks.

Or you could take your mom to the movies.

But maybe you'd rather save your money. If you leave your ten dollars in the bank for ten years, it will earn $6.40 in interest, and you will have $16.40.

If you leave it there for fifty years, your ten dollars will grow to $138.02.

YOU'VE WORKED HARD TO EARN
ONE HUNDRED DOLLARS.

You've decided to spend it on a plane ticket to the beach.
You could pay with a hundred-dollar bill, or two
fifty-dollar bills, or five twenty-dollar bills, or many other
combinations—six fives, three tens, and two twenties,
for instance.

Paying with pennies? You'll need ten thousand of them,
and they'll make a fifty-foot stack.

YOU'VE WORKED LONG AND HARD, AND YOU'VE EARNED A THOUSAND DOLLARS!

You're going to buy a pet. You could pay with coins or bills.

If you don't like the idea of carrying a thousand dollars around with you, you can put it in the bank and pay for the hippo with a check.

The check tells your bank to give $1,000 to the person who sold you the hippo.

GRACE
CHEERFUL AND WILLING INC.
Somewhere, U.S.A.

Pay to the order of ___ MR. HORACE HUGGABLE ___ $1,000.00

___ ONE THOUSAND and 0/100 Dollars

Grace

THE BANK
Somewhere, U.S.A.

Here's how it works: You give the check to the person who sold you the hippo, and he gives it to his bank, and his bank sends it to a very busy clearinghouse in the city, and the clearinghouse tells your bank to take $1,000 out of your money.

After your bank does that, the clearinghouse tells the hippo salesman's bank to add $1,000 to his money, so he can take it and use it whenever, and however, he likes. Maybe he'll use it to raise more hippos.

If you used pennies to purchase a $10,000 Ferris wheel, someone might not be too happy about it. Even if you used ten thousand one-dollar bills, they would be mighty hard to handle.

Probably a check would be best.

MAGNIFICENT!

YOU'VE EARNED $50,000. And you've just read about a
well-worn, unloved, but perfectly fixable castle for sale.
The price: $100,000.

The castle costs $100,000 and you have only $50,000.
You're $50,000 short, but you can still buy the castle.
You could use the money you earned as a down payment
and ask a bank to lend you the rest.

Then you would pay the bank back, a little at a time, month after month . . . for many years.

But the amount you must pay the bank will be *more* than what you borrowed. That's because the bank charges for lending you money. The extra money is called interest, just like the interest the bank pays to you when it uses your money. Now you are using the bank's money, so you must pay interest to the bank.

If you have some very expensive plans, you may have to take on a tough job that pays well.

If you think ogre-taming would be an exciting challenge, you can have fun and make a great deal of money, too. Of course, you may not enjoy taming obstreperous ogres or building bulky bridges or painting purple pots. Enjoying your work is more important than money, so you should look for another job or make less expensive plans.

CONGRATULATIONS!
YOU'VE MADE A MILLION.

A MILLION DOLLARS!

That's a stack of pennies ninety-five miles high, or enough nickels to fill a school bus, or a whale's weight in quarters.

Would you prefer your million in paper money? Even a paper million is a hefty load: A million one-dollar bills would weigh 2,500 pounds and stack up to 360 feet.

What's the smallest your million could be? One-hundred-dollar bills are the largest made today, and it would take ten thousand of them to pay you for your feat of ogre-taming.

But a check for $1,000,000 would easily fit in your pocket or purse. And it's worth the same as the towering stacks of pennies or bills.

Now you can afford to buy tickets to the moon.

Or you can purchase some real estate for the endangered rhinoceroses.

But if you'd rather save your million than spend it, you could put it in the bank, where it would earn interest. The interest on a million is about $1,000 a week, or $143 a day, or $6 an hour, or 10 cents a minute. Just from sitting in the bank!

If you keep your million, you can probably live on the interest without doing any more work for the rest of your life. You might like that, or you could find it rather dull.

Making money means
making choices.

SO WHAT WOULD YOU DO IF YOU MADE A MILLION?

THINK ABOUT IT

1. What are some reasons people put their money in a bank?

2. How does the author make it fun to learn and think about money? Give some examples.

3. What do you think the author means when he writes that making money means making choices? Explain your answer.

Imagine you wanted to write or illustrate a book that would be sold in bookstores. You would probably need an editor. An editor makes sure that a book is ready to be published. Here are some letters that David Schwartz and Steven Kellogg might have written to their editor.

From the Desk of
David M. Schwartz

Dear Editor:

My earlier book, *How Much Is a Million?*, is about large numbers. I have always liked thinking about large numbers. Sometimes I wonder if anyone could ever count all the stars in the sky. Some of my readers have told me they like to think about large numbers too, especially numbers like a million dollars!

This gave me an idea for a new book. A book for children about money would be great. After all, they will be earning, spending, and saving money all their lives.

I will send you a draft of what I have in mind for the new book. Please contact Mr. Steven Kellogg, and tell him about this project. I would love to have him illustrate this book.

Sincerely,

David M. Schwartz

David M. Schwartz

From the Desk of
Steven Kellogg

Dear Editor:

Thank you for writing to me about the new project. I am very interested in working on Mr. Schwartz's new book, *If You Had a Million*. I am already thinking about the illustrations.

I think it is a wonderful idea to make a book that will help children understand money. The book would be even better if it were more about *earning* money. We could change the title to *If You Made a Million*. I think it is important that people earn money by doing work they enjoy. Maybe this book will show children that they can help others, earn money, and have fun, all at the same time!

I will send you some sketches soon. I look forward to working with you and Mr. Schwartz again.

Sincerely,

Steven Kellogg

Steven Kellogg

Visit *The Learning Site!*
www.harcourtschool.com

Suppose you have made some money by doing a job. You might decide to spend the money. You might look at advertisements like the one below to help you decide what to buy. Look at the example on these pages to learn about some of the parts of an advertisement.

STUPENDOUS STICKER STORE

A slogan, or catchy phrase → "We Stick with You!"

Is your sticker collection too small? Would you like to have the biggest collection of all your friends?

Come to the Stupendous Sticker Store.

A fact that can be proved → We've been selling stickers for more than twenty years, and *we have thousands of stickers to choose from!*

An opinion that cannot be proved → At the Stupendous Sticker Store, we believe that *the biggest collection is the best collection.*

Let us help you make your collection as big as it can be!

Don't Take Just Our Word for It!

Listen to what **Stevie "Wheels" Smith**, famous skateboarding champ, says about Stupendous Stickers!

An endorsement, or statement of approval given by a famous person.

"Stupendous Stickers are the best!"

Meet
Stevie "Wheels" Smith
in person
at the Stupendous Sticker Store
on Saturday at 10 A.M.!

Think About It

What decisions do you have to make when reading an advertisement?

247

RESPONSE ACTIVITIES

SMART SHOPPER

COMPARE PRICES

Sometimes the same thing costs more in one store than another. Look through old newspapers. Find some advertisements for things that are the same, or almost the same. Paste the ads on a sheet of paper. Which item would you choose to buy? Explain to a classmate how you made your decision.

THANKS TO THE BANKS

WRITE A PARAGRAPH

Write a paragraph telling why banks are important in communities. Use facts from the selection. In your paragraph, explain how checks make money easier to handle. Also tell how people can earn money by using a bank. Read your paragraph aloud to a partner.

ALL THE SAME

Make a Chart

How many ways can you show $10 in coins and bills? Make a chart that shows five different ways. Draw rectangles for the bills and circles for the coins. Write the value of each bill or coin inside the shape. You might use your chart to help a younger child understand money.

MAKING CONNECTIONS

Create an Ad

The owner of Gloomsby Hall has hired you to write an advertisement that will attract buyers fast. The price is $100,000. Draw a picture and write words for your ad. Include a slogan and some opinions from famous people like the ones in the Stupendous Sticker Store ad.

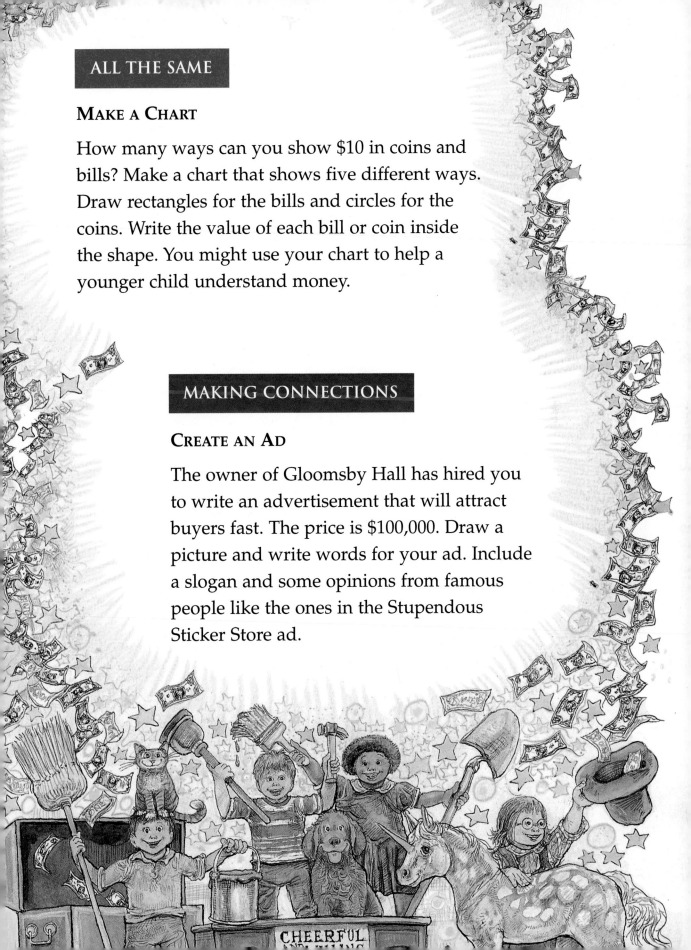

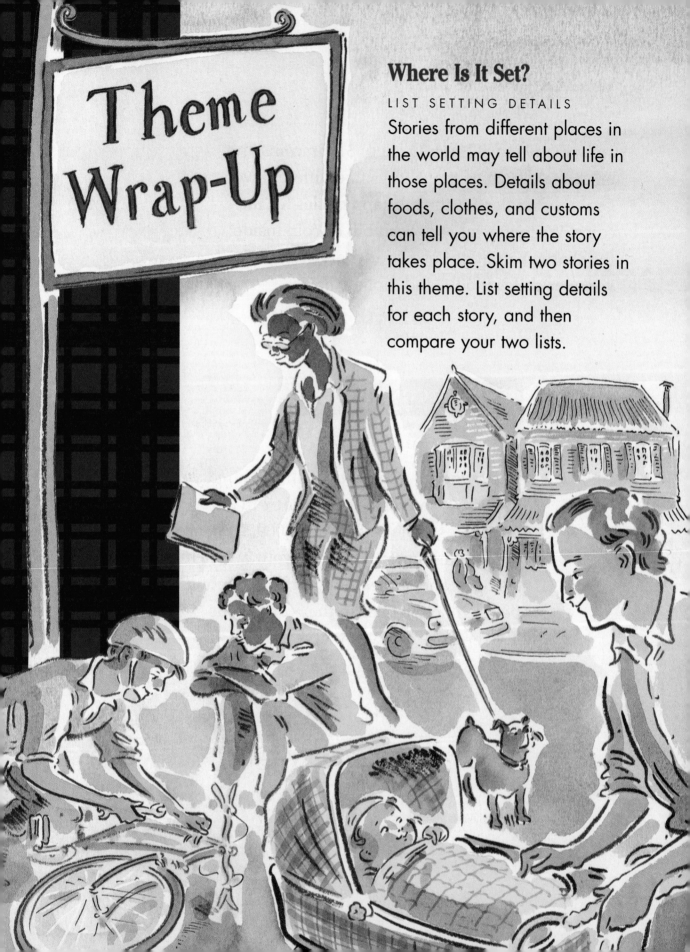

Theme Wrap-Up

Where Is It Set?

LIST SETTING DETAILS

Stories from different places in the world may tell about life in those places. Details about foods, clothes, and customs can tell you where the story takes place. Skim two stories in this theme. List setting details for each story, and then compare your two lists.

"Best of the Best" Awards

EXPRESS PERSONAL OPINIONS

Each selection in this theme is special in some way. Here's your chance to give each selection an award for being the "best of the best" in some way. First, decide what your awards will be for, such as the best pictures, the most interesting characters, or the most unusual setting. Then design ribbons or medals for the awards. Name the story that wins each award, and tell how you chose each winner.

What's the Solution?

MAKE DIAGRAM

The characters in the selections had problems to solve. Friends, family members, and other people helped them find solutions. Work in a small group to make a diagram that shows the problem in each selection and its solution. Here is an example.

Yippee-Yay!

Problem:	Solution:
Cattle owner must get cattle to market.	Cowboys ran cattle drives and earned money for their work.

Celebrate Our World

Contents

Reader's Choice

Earth: Our Planet in Space
by Seymour Simon
NONFICTION

Journey high above the Earth and see what causes summer and winter, day and night, and much more.

Award-Winning Author
READER'S CHOICE LIBRARY

Jordi's Star
by Alma Flor Ada
FANTASY

A star in a puddle is the beginning of a desert garden that grows into something much larger.

Award-Winning Author
READER'S CHOICE LIBRARY

So That's How the Moon Changes Shape!
by Allan Fowler

NONFICTION

From new moon to full moon, learn what's really happening.

Water Dance
by Thomas Locker

FREE VERSE/FINE ART

The wonder of water is all around us. It is light, it is dark; it is strong, it is gentle. Take another look!

Outstanding Science Trade Book; Teachers' Choice

Archibald Frisby
by Michael Chesworth

FICTION/RHYMED VERSE

Archibald is amazed at the world around him and shows his camp friends things they never noticed.

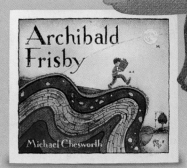

255

I'm in Charge of Celebrations

by *Byrd Baylor* ◆ pictures by *Peter Parnall*

Award-Winning Author and Illustrator

257

Sometimes
people ask me,
"Aren't you lonely
out there
with just
desert
around you?"

I guess they mean
the beargrass
and the yuccas
and the cactus
and the rocks.

I guess they mean
the deep ravines
and the hawk nests
in the cliffs
and the coyote trails
that wind
across the hills.

"Lonely?"

I can't help
laughing
when they ask me
that.

I always look at them . . .
surprised.

And I say,
"How could I be lonely?
I'm the one
in charge of
celebrations."

Sometimes
they don't believe me,
but it's true.
I am.

I put
myself
in charge.
I choose
my own.

Last year
I gave myself
one hundred and eight
celebrations—
besides the ones
that they close school for.

I cannot get by
with only
a few.

Friend, I'll tell you
how it works.

I keep a notebook
and I write the date
and then I write about
the celebration.

I'm very choosy
over
what goes in
that book.

It has to be something
I plan to remember
the rest of my life.

You can tell
what's worth
a celebration
because
your heart will
POUND
and
you'll feel
like you're standing
on top of a mountain
and you'll
catch your breath
like you were
breathing
some new kind of air.

Otherwise,
I count it just
an average day.
(I told you
I was
choosy.)

Friend, I wish you'd been here
for Dust Devil Day.

But since you weren't,
I'll tell you how
it got to be
my first
real
celebration.

You can call them
whirlwinds
if you want to.
Me, I think
dust devils
has a better sound.

Well, anyway,
I always stop
to watch them.
Here, everyone does.

You know how
they come
from far away,
moving
up from the flats,
swirling
and swaying
and falling

and turning,
picking up sticks
and sand
and feathers
and dry tumbleweeds.

Well, last March eleventh
we were all going somewhere.
I was in the back
of a pickup truck
when the dust devils
started
to gather.

You could see
they were
giants.

You'd swear
they were
calling
their friends
to come too.

And they came—
dancing
in time to
their own
windy music.

We all started counting.
We all started looking
for more.

They stopped that truck
and we turned
around
and around
watching them all.
There were seven.

At a time like that,
something
goes kind of crazy
in you.
You have to run
to meet them,
yelling
all the way.

You have to
whirl around
like you were
one of them,
and you can't stop
until
you're falling down.

And then all day
you think
how
lucky
you were
to be there.

Some of my best
celebrations
are sudden surprises
like that.

If you weren't outside
at that
exact
moment,
you'd miss them.

I spend a lot of time
outside
myself,
looking around.

Once
I saw a triple rainbow
that ended in a canyon
where I'd been
the day before.

I was halfway up a hill
standing
in a drizzle of rain.

It was almost dark
but I wouldn't go in
(because of the rainbows,
of course),
and there
at the top of the hill
a jackrabbit
was standing
up on his hind legs,
perfectly still,
looking straight
at that same
triple
rainbow.

I may be
the only person in the world
who's seen
a rabbit
standing in the mist
quietly watching
three rainbows.

That's worth
a celebration
any time.

I wrote it down
and drew the hill
and the rabbit
and the rainbow
and me.

Now
August ninth
is Rainbow Celebration Day.

I have
Green Cloud Day
too.

Ask anybody
and they'll tell you
clouds
aren't
green.

But
late one winter afternoon
I saw
this huge
green cloud.

It was not
bluish-green
or grayish-green
or something else.
This cloud
was
green . . .

green as a jungle parrot.

And the strange thing was
that it began
to take a parrot's shape,
first
the wings,
and then the head
and beak.

High in the winter sky
that green bird
flew.

It didn't last
more than a minute.
You know how fast
a cloud
can change,
but I still
remember
how it looked.

So I celebrate
green clouds
on February sixth.

263

At times like that,
I always think,
"What if I'd missed it?
What if I'd been
in the house?
Or what if I hadn't
looked up
when I did?"

You can see I'm
very lucky
about things
like that.

And
I was lucky
on Coyote Day,
because
out of all time
it had to be
one moment
only
that
a certain coyote
and I
could meet—
and we did.

Friend, you should have
been here too.

I was following
deer tracks,
taking my time,
bending down
as I walked,
kind of humming.
(I hum a lot
when I'm alone.)

I looked up
in time to see
a young coyote
trotting
through the brush.

She crossed
in front of me.
It was a windy day
and she was going east.

In that easy
silent way
coyotes move,
she pushed
into the wind.

I stood there
hardly breathing,
wishing I
could move
that way.

I was surprised
to see her
stop
and turn
and look
at me.

She seemed to think
that I was
just
another
creature
following another
rocky trail.

(That's true, of course.
I am.)

She didn't hurry.
She wasn't afraid.

I saw her eyes
and she saw
mine.

That look
held us
together.

Because of that,
I never will
feel
quite the same
again.

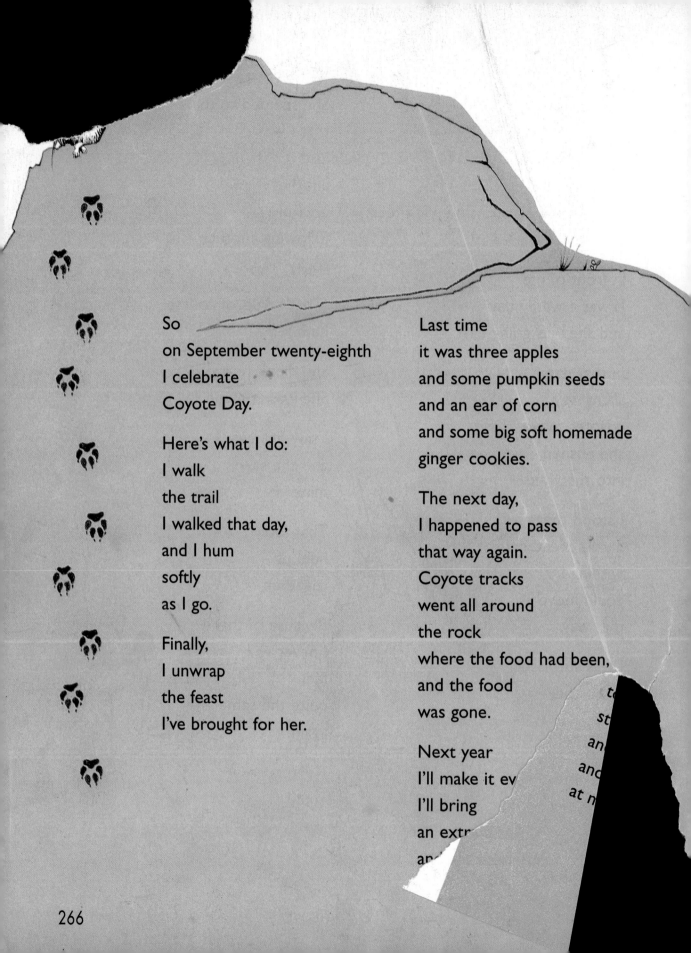

So
on September twenty-eighth
I celebrate
Coyote Day.

Here's what I do:
I walk
the trail
I walked that day,
and I hum
softly
as I go.

Finally,
I unwrap
the feast
I've brought for her.

Last time
it was three apples
and some pumpkin seeds
and an ear of corn
and some big soft homemade
ginger cookies.

The next day,
I happened to pass
that way again.
Coyote tracks
went all around
the rock
where the food had been,
and the food
was gone.

Next year
I'll make it ev
I'll bring
an extr
an

Another one
of my greatest
of all celebrations
is called
The Time of Falling Stars.

It lasts
almost a week
in the middle
of August,
and I wait
all year
for those hot
summer nights
when the sky
goes
wild.

You can call them
meteor showers
if you want to.
Me, I like to say
they're
falling stars.

All that week
I sleep outside.

I give
my full attention
to the sky.

And every time
a streak of light
goes
shooting
through the darkness,
I feel my heart
shoot
out of me.

One night
I saw
a fireball
that left
a long
red
blazing
trail
across the sky.

After it was
gone,
I stood there
looking up,
not quite
believing
what I'd seen.

The strange thing was,
I met a man
who told me
he had seen it too
while he was lying
by a campfire
five hundred miles
away.

He said he did not sleep
again
that night.

Suddenly
it seemed
that we two
spoke a language
no one else
could
understand.

Every August
of my life,
I'll think of that.

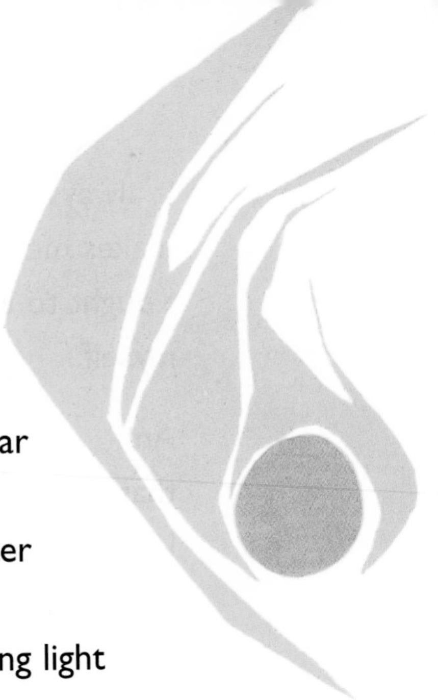

Friend,
I've saved
my New Year Celebration
until last.

Mine
is a little
different
from the one
most people have.

It comes in
spring.

To tell the truth,
I never did
feel like
my new year
started
January first.

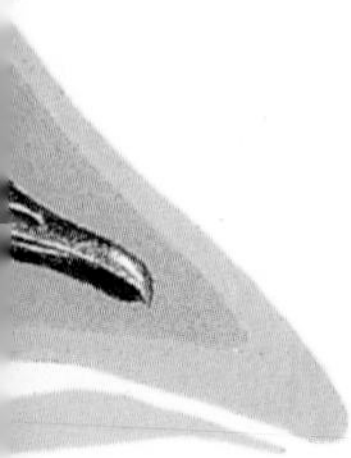

To me,
that's just
another
winter day.

I let my year
begin
when winter
ends
and morning light
comes
earlier,
the way it *should*.

That's when
I feel like
starting
new.

I wait
until
the white-winged doves
are back from Mexico,
and wildflowers
cover the hills,
and my favorite
cactus
blooms.

It always
makes me think
I ought to bloom
myself.

And
that's when
I start to plan
my New Year
Celebration.

I finally choose
a day
that is
exactly
right.

Even the air
has to be
perfect,
and the dirt
has to feel
good and warm
on bare feet.

(Usually,
it's a Saturday
around the end
of April.)

I have a drum
that I beat
to signal
The Day.

Then I go
wandering off,
following all
of my favorite
trails
to all of the
places
I like.

I check how
everything
is doing.

I spend the day
admiring
things.

If the old desert tortoise
I know from last year
is out
strolling around,
I'll go his direction
awhile.

I celebrate
with horned toads
and ravens
and lizards
and quail. . . .

And, Friend,
it's not
a bad
party.

Walking back home
(kind of humming),
sometimes
I think about
those people
who ask me if
I'm *lonely* here.

I have to
laugh
out
loud.

Think About It

1 What is similar about all of the celebration days the author describes?

2 Which day in the story would you choose for a celebration day? Explain why.

3 Why does the author laugh out loud when people ask if she is lonely?

Meet the Author

Byrd Baylor

Dear Friends,

I'm in Charge of Celebrations is about my life and my home. I was born in Texas, and I spent many summers on a West Texas ranch. I love living where I can see cactus and red cliffs. I love hearing coyotes on cold, clear nights. These are the things I celebrate.

You can celebrate nature, too. Listen to the birds, and look at the flowers and the stones. Feel the wind and the sun and the rain. There are so many reasons to celebrate!

Yours truly,

Byrd Baylor

Meet the Illustrator Peter Parnall

Dear Readers,

I love to study nature, especially animals. I almost became a veterinarian, but I decided I liked drawing animals more than doctoring them. I have been very happy drawing pictures for other authors' books. I have also written and illustrated some of my own books.

I now live and work on a farm in Maine. I enjoy taking long walks in the woods near the farm and sharing my art with children. I hope you enjoyed my pictures in *I'm in Charge of Celebrations*.

Yours truly,

Peter Parnall

Visit *The Learning Site!*
www.harcourtschool.com

Response Activities

WHAT A DAY!

WRITE A JOURNAL ENTRY

The girl in the poem records all the wonderful things she sees by writing about them in a book. Sometimes she also draws what she has seen. Choose one of the days she talks about, or one of your own special days. Write a journal entry for that day. You may wish to add a drawing to your entry.

A NATURE POEM

WRITE A POEM

The poem "I'm in Charge of Celebrations" is about the desert. Write your own poem about an outdoor place that you enjoy. You might write about a park, a beach, or a yard. Describe the colors, smells, and sounds of your place so that your readers can imagine it.

QUIET MOTION

WRITE AN OBSERVATION

The narrator talks about "that easy silent way coyotes move." Choose an animal to watch. It may be a pet, a bird in the wild, or an animal in a nature film. Pay attention to the way it moves and acts. Write a paragraph telling what you learned about the animal by watching it move.

DESERT MOVES

MAKE UP A DANCE

Make up a dance to celebrate desert life. Your dance could show how coyotes move or what whirlwinds look like. Set your dance to music, and perform it for some classmates.

Important Details

You know that the main idea is what a story or paragraph is mostly about. **Details** are pieces of information that tell more about the main idea. Read this paragraph about Byrd Baylor.

> Byrd Baylor, an author of children's books, loves her home. She lives in the state of Arizona, in the desert. She loves the beauty of the desert. The rough and rocky mountains, the bright stars, and the red sunsets make her feel happy. On cold nights she enjoys the sound of coyotes.

To find the important details in the paragraph, you can ask yourself questions.

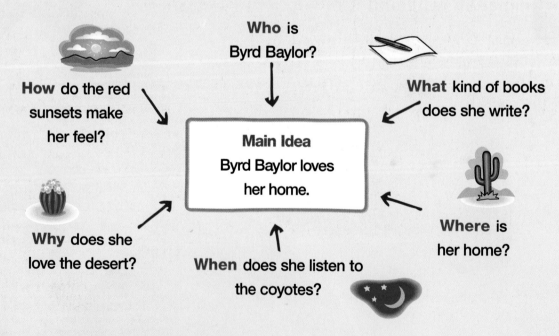

Who is Byrd Baylor?

How do the red sunsets make her feel?

What kind of books does she write?

Main Idea
Byrd Baylor loves her home.

Why does she love the desert?

When does she listen to the coyotes?

Where is her home?

Finding important details can help you understand the author's main idea. In a story, details often give information about the characters, settings, and events.

Read the paragraph below. Try answering questions that start with *Who*, *What*, *Where*, *When*, *Why*, and *How*.

Spring is Mike's favorite season. The weather starts to get warm, and he does not have to wear a jacket. He can play outside longer with his friends. School is fun in spring, too. Last spring his class went on a field trip to a farm. The students fed the young ducklings and helped plant seeds.

WHAT HAVE YOU LEARNED?

1. Why should readers pay attention to important details?

2. What is your favorite time of year? Give some details about what makes it special for you.

Visit *The Learning Site!* www.harcourtschool.com

TRY THIS • TRY THIS • TRY THIS

Reread the paragraph above. Draw a web to show the main idea and the details.

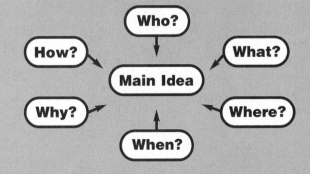

BY RICHARD E. ALBERT
ILLUSTRATED BY SYLVIA LONG

ALEJANDRO'S GIFT

Alejandro's small adobe house stood beside a lonely desert road.

Beside the house stood a well, and a windmill to pump water from the well. Water for Alejandro and for his only companion, a burro.

It was a lonely place, and Alejandro welcomed any who stopped by to refresh themselves at the well. But visitors were few, and after they left, Alejandro felt lonelier than before.

To more easily endure the lonely hours, Alejandro planted a garden. A garden filled with carrots, beans, and large brown onions.

Tomatoes and corn.

Melons, squash, and small red peppers.

Most mornings found Alejandro tending the garden, watching it grow. These were times he cherished, and he often stayed for hours, working until driven indoors by the desert heat.

The days went by, one after another with little change, until one morning when there was an unexpected visitor. This visitor came not from the desert road, but from the desert itself.

A ground squirrel crept from the underbrush. Moving
warily over the sand, it hesitated and looked around. Alejandro
paused, keeping very quiet as the squirrel approached the
garden. It ran up to one of the furrows, drank its fill of water,
and scampered away. After it left, Alejandro realized that for
those few moments his loneliness had been all but forgotten.

And because he felt less lonely, Alejandro found himself
hoping the squirrel would come again.

The squirrel did come again, from time to time bringing
along small friends.

Wood rats and pocket gophers.

Jackrabbits, kangaroo rats, pocket mice.

Birds, too, became aware of Alejandro's garden.

Roadrunners, gila woodpeckers, thrashers.

Cactus wrens, sage sparrows, mourning doves, and others came in the evening to perch on the branches of a mesquite bush, or to rest on the arms of a lone saguaro, before dropping down for a quick drink before nightfall.

Occasionally, even an old desert tortoise could be seen plodding toward the garden.

Suddenly, Alejandro found that time was passing more quickly. He was rarely lonely. He had only to look up from his hoe, or from wherever he might be at any moment, to find a small friend nearby.

For a while this was all that mattered to Alejandro, but after a time he wasn't so sure. He began asking himself if there was something more important than just making himself less lonely. It took Alejandro little time to see there was.

He began to realize that his
tiny desert friends came to his garden not
for company, but for water. And he found himself thinking
of the other animals in the desert.

Animals like the coyote and the desert gray fox.

The bobcats, the skunks, the badgers, the long-nosed coatis.

The peccaries, sometimes called *javelinas*, the short-
tempered wild pigs of the desert.

The antlered mule deer, the does, and the fawns.

Finding enough water was not a problem. With his windmill
and well, Alejandro could supply ample water for any and all.
Getting it to those who needed it was something else.

The something else, Alejandro decided, was a desert water hole.

Without delay, Alejandro started digging. It was tiring work, taking many days in the hot desert sun. But the thought of giving water to so many thirsty desert dwellers more than made up for the drudgery. And when it was filled, Alejandro was pleased with the gift he had made for his desert friends.

There was good reason to suppose it would take time for the larger animals to discover their new source of water, so

Alejandro was patient. He went about as usual, feeding his burro, tending the garden, and doing countless other chores.

Days passed and nothing happened. Still, Alejandro was confident. But the days turned to weeks, and it was still quiet at the water hole. Why, Alejandro wondered, weren't they coming? What could he have done wrong?

The absence of the desert folk might have remained a mystery had Alejandro not come out of the house one morning when a skunk was in the clearing beyond the water hole. Seeing Alejandro, the skunk darted to safety in the underbrush.

It suddenly became very clear why Alejandro's gift was being shunned.

Alejandro couldn't believe he had been so thoughtless, but what was important now was to put things right as quickly as possible.

Water hole number two was built far from the house and screened by heavy desert growth. When it was filled and ready, Alejandro waited with mixed emotions. He was hopeful, yet he couldn't forget what had happened the first time.

As it turned out, he was not disappointed.

The animals of the desert did come, each as it made its own discovery. Because the water hole was now sheltered from the small adobe house and the desert road, the animals were no longer fearful. And although Alejandro could not see through

the desert growth surrounding the water hole, he had ways of knowing it was no longer being shunned.

By the twitter of birds gathering in the dusk.

By the rustling of mesquite in the quiet desert evening telling of the approach of a coyote, a badger, or maybe a desert fox.

By the soft hoofbeats of a mule deer, or the unmistakable sound of a herd of peccaries charging toward the water hole.

And in these moments when Alejandro sat quietly listening to the sounds of his desert neighbors, he knew that the gift was not so much a gift that he had given, but a gift he had received.

THINK ABOUT IT

1 Alejandro had a well. Why did he dig the two water holes?

2 Do you think having animals nearby can help people who are lonely? Explain your answer.

3 What is the *gift* in the story title?

Meet the Author
Richard E. Albert

Richard E. Albert spent most of his life working as an engineer for a gas company. He wrote some Western stories, as well as stories for children's magazines. Then, when he was eighty-three, he wrote *Alejandro's Gift*. It was the first book he had written for children.

Meet the Illustrator
Sylvia Long

Drawing and horses were always on Sylvia Long's mind when she was a child. Her favorite birthday presents were crayons, paints, and pencils. She also wished for a horse on every birthday. Finally she got her own horse after she was married.

Today Sylvia Long lives in Arizona and draws pictures for magazines and picture books. She says that she feels "so lucky to be able to draw and call it work."

Visit *The Learning Site!*
www.harcourtschool.com

THIS LAND IS YOUR LAND

words and music by Woody Guthrie

Trail Riders, **Thomas Hart Benton**
1964/1965. Polymer tempera on canvas 56 ⅛ in. x 74 in. National Gallery of Art, Washington, D.C.

294

CHORUS

This land is your land,___ This land is my land,___ from Cal - i -
for - nia ___ to the New York is - land;___ From the red - wood
for - est ___ to the Gulf Stream wa - ters ___

1. (to Verses) (Fine)

This land was made for you and me.___ me.___

As I was walking that ribbon of highway,
I saw above me that endless skyway;
I saw below me that golden valley:
This land was made for you and me.

I've roamed and rambled and I followed my footsteps
To the sparkling sands of her diamond deserts;
And all around me a voice was sounding:
This land was made for you and me.

When the sun came shining, and I was strolling,
And the wheat fields waving and the dust clouds rolling,
As the fog was lifting a voice was chanting:
This land was made for you and me.

RESPONSE ACTIVITIES

In Alejandro's Words

WRITE A JOURNAL ENTRY

The first day the animals start coming to the watering hole is special for Alejandro. If Alejandro wrote about it, what do you think he would say? Write a journal entry that he might write. Tell what happens and how he feels about it.

Cheer Up!

MAKE A LIST

Alejandro feels lonely, so he builds a watering hole to invite animal visitors. With a partner, think of other things a person could do to feel less lonely. Make a list, and share it with some classmates.

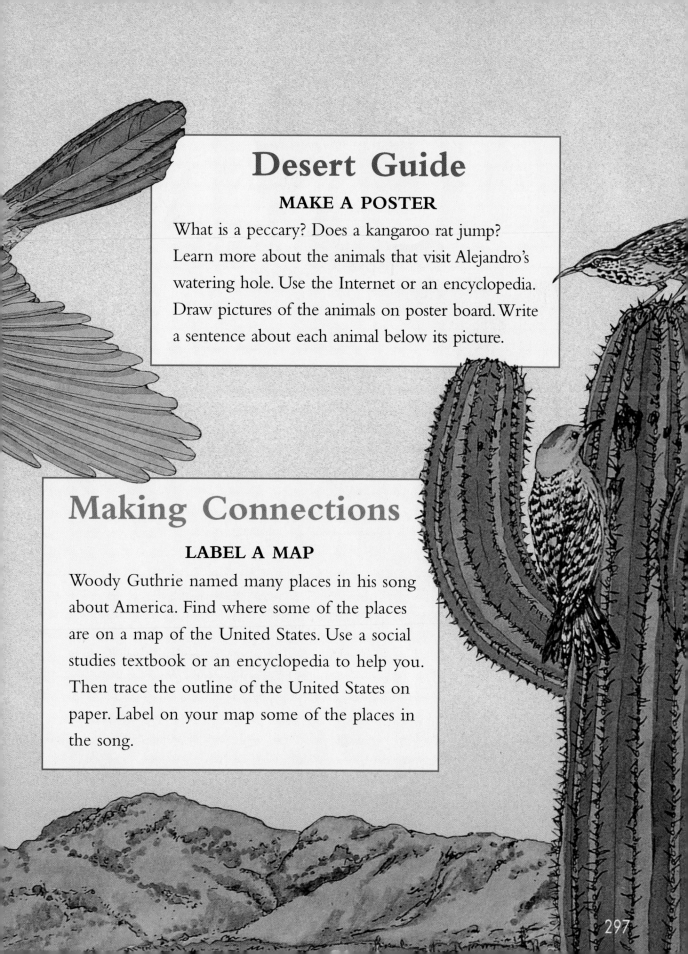

Desert Guide

MAKE A POSTER

What is a peccary? Does a kangaroo rat jump?
Learn more about the animals that visit Alejandro's
watering hole. Use the Internet or an encyclopedia.
Draw pictures of the animals on poster board. Write
a sentence about each animal below its picture.

Making Connections

LABEL A MAP

Woody Guthrie named many places in his song
about America. Find where some of the places
are on a map of the United States. Use a social
studies textbook or an encyclopedia to help you.
Then trace the outline of the United States on
paper. Label on your map some of the places in
the song.

ROCKING AND

by Philip Steele

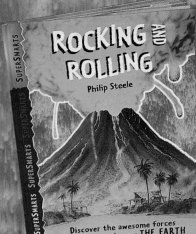

ROCKING AND
ROLLING

Philip Steele

Discover the awesome forces
that shape and move THE EARTH

DOWN UNDER

Our planet Earth is huge—about 3,960 miles from the surface to the center. Walking this far would take you about 55 days and nights.

You wouldn't be able to walk to the center of the earth, though, as it's incredibly hot. It's at least 9,000°F, which is nearly the same temperature as the surface of the sun.

Outer core

Inner core

Earth has four layers. The top one is called the crust and it's made of rock. It's about 25 miles thick under the land, but only about 5 miles thick beneath the ocean.

The mantle is next. It's also made of rock, but it's so hot that some parts have melted into magma and are as gooey as oatmeal.

Beneath the mantle is Earth's core. This is made of metal and has two layers—an outer and an inner core.

The outer core is runny because it's so hot. But although the inner core is even hotter, it's solid. Why? Because the other three layers are pressing down on it and the weight is enough to squash it solid!

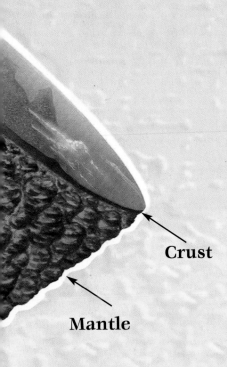

Crust

Mantle

People have always dreamed of digging down to the earth's center. But so far no one has invented a machine that would survive the heat.

CRACKING UP

If all the oceans disappeared, Earth would look just like a jigsaw puzzle made up of lots of big pieces.

The pieces are called plates, and there are about 20 of them. They float on the lower part of the earth's mantle, moving very, very slowly—between 1 and 8 inches per year.

Sometimes the plates move apart and gooey magma rises up from the mantle to fill the gap. The magma cools and hardens to form new land or ocean floor.

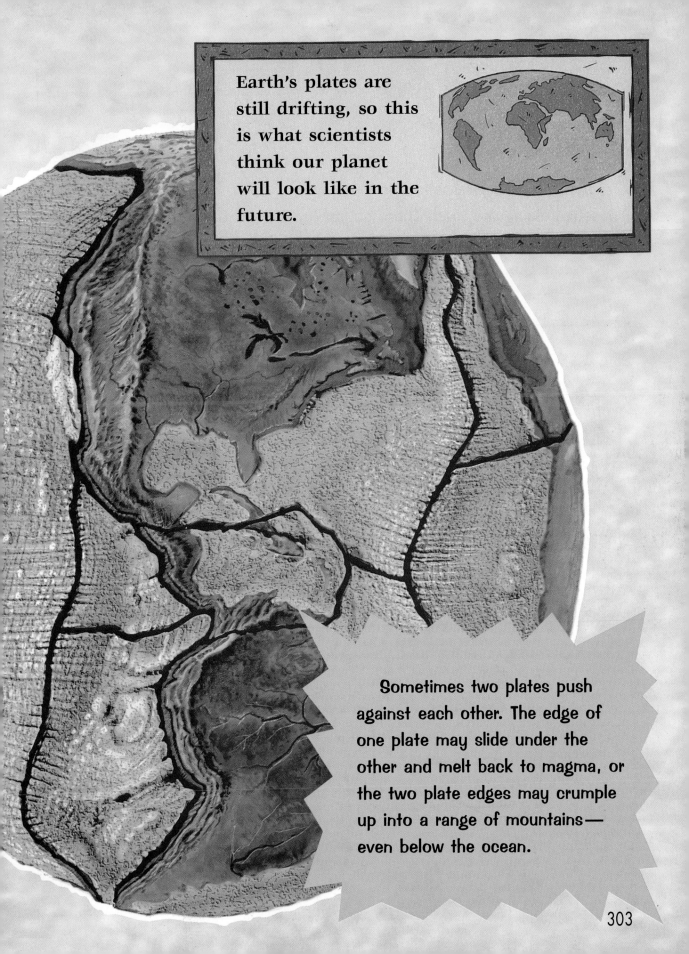

Earth's plates are still drifting, so this is what scientists think our planet will look like in the future.

Sometimes two plates push against each other. The edge of one plate may slide under the other and melt back to magma, or the two plate edges may crumple up into a range of mountains—even below the ocean.

QUAKE AND

Just a few minutes ago this truck was speeding along the road. Then, suddenly, there was a terrifying roar, and the ground opened up— an earthquake!

The most serious earthquakes happen deep underground, along the edges of the earth's plates.

Usually, the plates stay jammed close together. But from time to time a plate breaks away.

This makes the ground shudder and shake. Sometimes it can even split wide open.

SHAKE

These shudders can be felt thousands of miles away because they spread out from the earthquake's epicenter like the ripples from a stone thrown into a pond.

Every year, there are 40,000 to 50,000 earthquakes that are strong enough to be felt. However, only about 40 of them are big enough to cause any damage.

In Japan there's a National Disaster Prevention Day each year, when everyone practices what to do during an earthquake. Volunteers spend the day learning how to rescue people from fallen buildings.

WALLS OF

Most waves are made by the wind blowing over the sea. This is no ordinary wave, though. It's called a tsunami, and it was started by an earthquake.

A big earthquake is a lot like a huge bomb going off. The force of the explosion can create a tsunami that travels thousands of miles through the ocean.

When the tsunami is in deep ocean water, its top may be only 8–12 inches above the surface.

But as it rolls on into shallower water near the coast, the tsunami is forced upward into a gigantic wall of water— sometimes it can be even higher than an apartment building!

WATER

HIGHER AND HIGHER

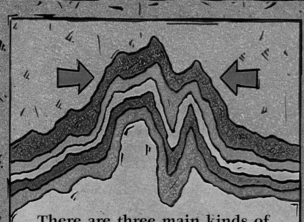

There are three main kinds of mountains. Fold mountains, like the Himalayas, form when the earth's plates crunch into one another, and layers of the crust are pushed up into loops and bumps.

Dome mountains happen when magma bulges up beneath the crust. This forces the crust up into a large rounded hump—much like the back of an elephant!

Block mountains are made when part of the crust is forced up between two cracks in a plate. These cracks are called faults.

Welcome to the top of the world. The Himalayas are the highest mountain ranges on Earth, and the tallest Himalayan peak is Mount Everest.

Everest already soars to a height of 29,029 feet. But next year it will be a tiny bit higher—it's still growing.

The Himalayas started forming around 53 million years ago when the earth's plate carrying the land that is now India began crunching upward into the rest of Asia.

Inch by inch, India pushed northward. And over tens of millions of years, the plate edges crumpled into the huge ridges, peaks, and valleys we see today.

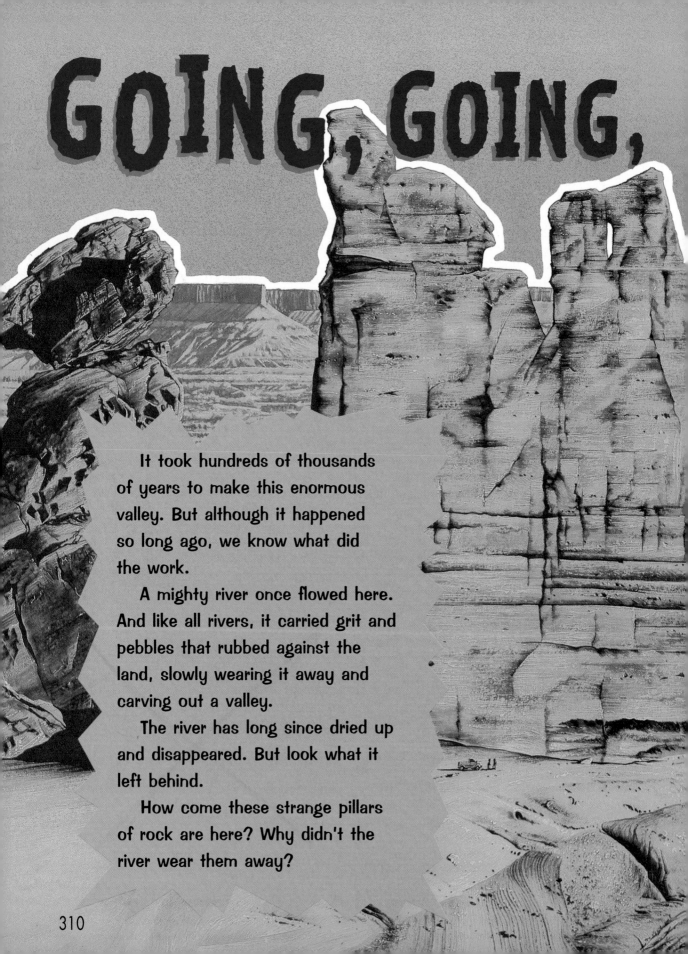

GOING, GOING,

It took hundreds of thousands of years to make this enormous valley. But although it happened so long ago, we know what did the work.

A mighty river once flowed here. And like all rivers, it carried grit and pebbles that rubbed against the land, slowly wearing it away and carving out a valley.

The river has long since dried up and disappeared. But look what it left behind.

How come these strange pillars of rock are here? Why didn't the river wear them away?

GONE!

Well, some rocks are harder than others, and hard rocks break down more slowly than soft ones. The river dried up before it had time to wear these pillars away.

The wearing away of the land is called erosion, and it's still going on today. But water isn't doing the work now—so what is?

The answer is blowing in the wind. Day after day it whistles through the valley, picking up grit and sand and blasting everything it touches.

The wind works like sandpaper, slowly wearing the rocks down and grinding them into weird and wonderful shapes.

Rock is much harder than wind and water—yet given time, wind and water are powerful enough to shape the land we live on.

Think About It

1 Will Earth look the same in one million years as it does now? How do you know?

2 What is one fact you learned from "Rocking and Rolling" that you did not know before?

3 How is this nonfiction selection different from a story?

MEET THE AUTHOR PHILIP STEELE

Philip Steele would make an interesting employee. Look over this application. What information might tell you that he is a good writer? Would you hire him to write for you?

Application for Employment

Name Philip Steele	Job Desired Author
Address Ynys Môn, Wales, United Kingdom	

Education   University College, Durham

Work History
English teacher, Germany
Editor for educational books, London, England
Writer and editor, North Wales

Hobbies   Traveling, backpacking
Other Languages   Welsh

Special Skills and Interests
I am curious and want to learn new things.
I enjoy history and nature. I also visit local
schools to keep in touch with children's interests.

Published Works
The Greek News
The Blue Whale
The People Atlas

Visit *The Learning Site!*
www.harcourtschool.com

(Do you have another sheet of paper so
that I can list all of them?)

RESPONSE

MOVERS AND SHAPERS

DRAW A DIAGRAM

This selection tells about forces that move and shape the land. Draw a diagram to help explain one of these forces. For example, draw a picture of an earthquake or of a mountain being formed. Add labels to show what is happening and what the parts of the land are called.

HOW FAR IS IT?

ESTIMATE DISTANCES

The distance from the surface of the Earth to its center is 3,969 miles (6,387 km). Estimate the distances from your town or city to other towns or cities that you have visited or would like to visit. Then look in an atlas or an encyclopedia to check how close you were. Compare your estimates with those of classmates.

ACTIVITIES

THE GREAT ESCAPE

WRITE A PLAY

Imagine that you and some of your classmates are caught in a tsunami, an earthquake, or another disaster. Write a short play about how you escape. Use information from "Rocking and Rolling" to help you describe the danger. Perform your play for other students.

ROCK HUNT

WRITE A REPORT

The Earth's crust is made up of three kinds of rock. Find out what the three kinds of rock are called. Write a report that tells how each kind is formed. Look for information in encyclopedias or science books.

315

Cause and Effect

"**R**ocking and Rolling" tells what happens when the earth's plates move. Often one thing makes something else happen. The reason an event happens is the **cause.** What happens is the **effect.** When you read, finding causes and effects helps you understand why events happen or why characters act as they do.

The chart below shows causes and effects in "Rocking and Rolling."

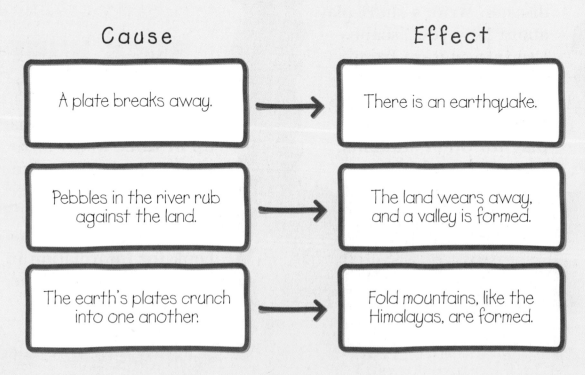

Cause	Effect
A plate breaks away.	There is an earthquake.
Pebbles in the river rub against the land.	The land wears away, and a valley is formed.
The earth's plates crunch into one another.	Fold mountains, like the Himalayas, are formed.

Finding causes and effects can help you understand what you read. To find an effect, ask "What happened?" To find a cause, ask "Why did it happen?" You can also look for words like *so, because,* and *therefore.* These words give you clues to causes and effects.

Read the paragraph below. Can you find a cause and an effect?

This mountain of sand in the desert is called a dune. Dunes are formed when wind blows across the desert and piles the sand high. The sand moves easily because there are no plants to keep it in place.

WHAT HAVE YOU LEARNED?

1. A newspaper reported that a building was flooded because a water pipe broke. What was the cause? What was the effect?

2. Tell what you think the effect would be if the electricity suddenly went off in your school. You may think of more than one effect.

Visit *The Learning Site!*
www.harcourtschool.com

TRY THIS • TRY THIS • TRY THIS

Think of something good that has happened to you. Draw a chart like the one below. In the box on the left, write the cause of what happened. Then write the effect in the box on the right.

Cause ⟶ Effect

THE
ARMADILLO
FROM
AMARILLO

WRITTEN AND ILLUSTRATED
LYNNE
CHERRY

Award-Winning
Author/Illustrator

The
from

TEXAS ARMADILLO
This burrowing mammal is covered with a bony shell. When attacked, the armadillo may roll up like a ball and depend upon its own armor for protection. Armadillos feed on fruits, roots, and insects.

SAN ANTONIO, TX
P.M
25 APR
1993

Dear Brillo,
I've lately had the urge to go and visit San Antonio, a city I've not seen before that my friends tell me I'd adore. ♡
Sasparillo

BRILLO ARMADILLO
PHILADELP
CHILDREN'S
3400 W. G
PHILA
PA

Distributed by Austin News Agency, Austin Texas

Plastichrome
Post mark

BLUEBONNETS
SAN ANTONIO
TEXAS

SAN ANTONIO
P.M
APR 14
1993

Dear Brillo,
Hi and warm regards from your cousin Sasparillo. I lay my head and slept today on a blue bluebonnet pillow.
Love,
Sasparillo

BRILLO AR
PHILADELPHIA
CHILDREN'S
3400 W. GIRARD
PHILADELP
PA 1910

Armadillo Amarillo

Written and Illustrated by Lynne Cherry

An Armadillo from Texas wondered,
"Where in the world am I?
What's out beyond these tangled woods?
What's out beyond the sky?"

So Armadillo packed up his things
and left his home behind.
He headed off on a northeast course
to seek what he could find.

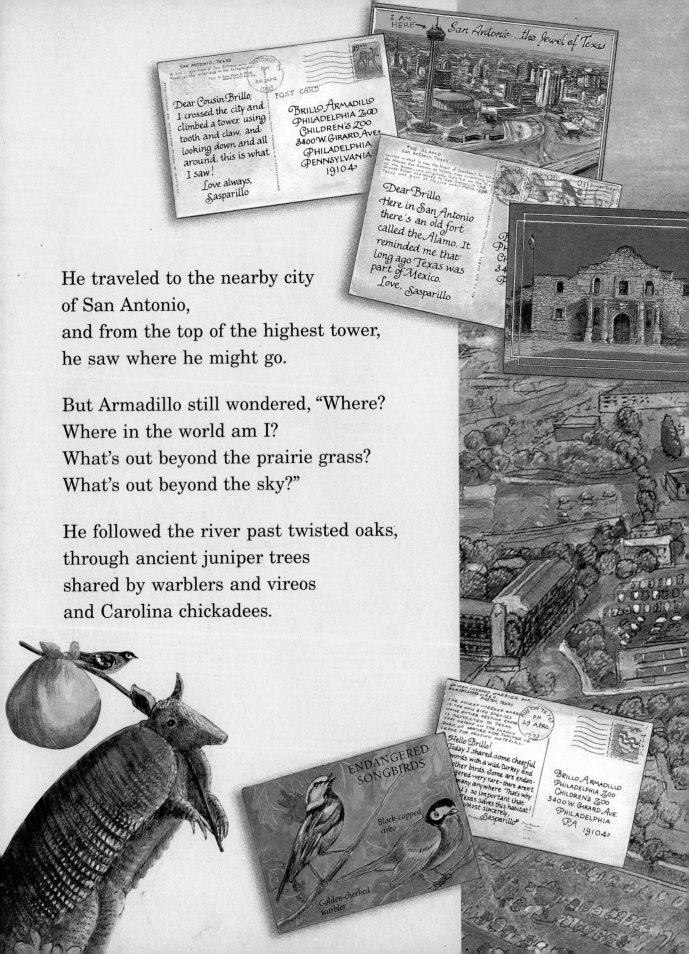

Dear Cousin Brillo,
I crossed the city and
climbed a tower, using
tooth and claw, and
looking down and all
around, this is what
I saw!
Love always,
Sasparillo

POST CARD

BRILLO ARMADILLO
PHILADELPHIA ZOO
CHILDREN'S ZOO
3400 W. GIRARD AVE.
PHILADELPHIA
PENNSYLVANIA
19104

San Antonio...the Jewel of Texas

I AM
HERE →

Dear Brillo,
Here in San Antonio
there's an old fort
called the Alamo. It
reminded me that
long ago Texas was
part of Mexico.
Love, Sasparillo

He traveled to the nearby city
of San Antonio,
and from the top of the highest tower,
he saw where he might go.

But Armadillo still wondered, "Where?
Where in the world am I?
What's out beyond the prairie grass?
What's out beyond the sky?"

He followed the river past twisted oaks,
through ancient juniper trees
shared by warblers and vireos
and Carolina chickadees.

ENDANGERED
SONGBIRDS

Black-capped
vireo

Golden-cheeked
warbler

Hello Brillo!
Today I shared some cheerful
words with a wild turkey, and
other birds. Some are endangered—very rare—there aren't
many anywhere. That's why
it's so important that
Texas saves this habitat!
Most sincerely,
Sasparillo

BRILLO ARMADILLO
PHILADELPHIA ZOO
CHILDREN'S ZOO
3400 W. GIRARD AVE.
PHILADELPHIA
PA 19104

The landscape changed dramatically
through woodland, towns, and plains.
Armadillo explored canyons
and walked through heavy rains.

He walked for weeks and came to Austin,
continued west and north
to Abilene and Lubbock,
he hiked and sallied forth.

Armadillo often along the way
climbed up to higher ground.
He scurried up the canyon walls
and stopped to look around.

How different were the plains above—
flowers went on for a mile!
Armadillo decided to settle down
and stay there for a while.

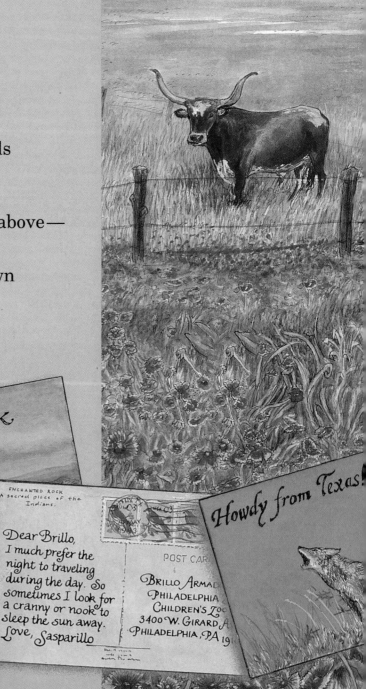

ENCHANTED ROCK
AUSTIN, TEXAS

ENCHANTED ROCK
A sacred place of the
Indians.

Dear Brillo,
I much prefer the
night to traveling
during the day. So
sometimes I look for
a cranny or nook to
sleep the sun away.
Love, Sasparillo

POST CARD

BRILLO ARMA___
PHILADELPHIA
CHILDREN'S ZOO
3400 W. GIRARD A___
PHILADELPHIA, PA 19___

Howdy from Texas!

Dear Brillo,
I'm near Amarillo.
This land is cool and
flat! It's definitely
an inadequate
Armadillo habitat!
I'll be the only
Armadillo who lives
near the city of
Amarillo!
♥ Sasparillo

POST CARD

BRILLO ARMADILLO
PHILADELPHIA ZOO
CHILDREN'S ZOO
3400 W. GIRARD AVE.
PHILADELPHIA, PA
19104

But Armadillo still wondered, "Where?
Where in the world *am* I?
Perhaps I'd have a better idea
if I could somehow fly."

One day he asked the golden eagle
as she came breezing by,
"What can I do for a bird's-eye view
from up in the big blue sky?"

"Hop on my back," said the eagle.
"I'll fly you wide and far.
And then you'll see, eventually,
where in the world we are."

Upward and upward the eagle flew.
Armadillo held on tight.
"With my tail-tip curled I'll explore the world
from morning until night!"

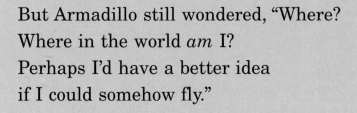

Palo Duro
Canyon
Amarillo,
TEXAS

PALO DURO CANYON
New Amarillo and Canyon Texas
The Lighthouse The Best Known Formation
in Palo Duro Canyon State Park

Dear Brillo,
Except for the canyons like
this one here, this land is
flat, flat, flat! And
an Armadillo near
Amarillo should wear
a scarf and hat!
Love,
Sasparillo

POST CARD

BRILLO ARMADILLO
PHILADELPHIA ZOO
CHILDREN'S ZOO
3400 W. GIRARD AVE.
PHILADELPHIA, PA
19104

Armadillo looked down below and asked,
"Where in the world *are* we?"
"We're over a prairie, and in the distance,
that's Amarillo you see.

"We've flown over the prairie.
We've flown over a town.
Amarillo means yellow, my dear little fellow,
and the prairie's all yellow and brown!"

"I see Amarillo," said Armadillo.
"Could we see all Texas, though?
And if we fly *higher* up into the sky,
could we see New Mexico?

"Or if we fly *higher* up into the sky,
could we see the entire earth?"
"Well, certainly, surely, if you hold on securely,
we'll try!" cried the eagle with mirth.

"*Amarillo*'s a *city?*" asked Armadillo.
To this the eagle replied,
"Yes, Amarillo's a city in *Texas*,
the *state* where we reside.

"And Texas is in the *United States*,
our *country* wide and dear,
on the *North American continent*,
which is on the *earth*, a sphere.

"This sphere is called a *planet*,
of nine we are just one,
and as we converse, in the *universe*,
these planets turn round the sun."

Armadillo held tightly to Eagle's neck,
afraid of a long, long fall.
From over his shoulder, with the air getting colder,
this is what he saw.

They flew so high up into the sky
that Texas they saw below—
the part they call the Panhandle—
and the state of New Mexico.

"With my tail-tip curled I'll explore the world!"
Armadillo said to his friend.
Through the clouds they twirled, in the wind
they whirled, and up they were hurled again!

And when they looked up they could see into space.
They'd flown up into thin air.
"It's hard to breathe here! I'd like to leave here!
Eagle, homeward let's repair!"

"We're very high now," said Eagle,
"on the edge of air and space.
The atmosphere's ending, we should be descending,
but what a remarkable place!"

"There must be a way to fly higher up,
bringing some air aboard.
Perhaps we should travel to Cape Canaveral,"
Eagle said as she soared.

As they spoke of Cape Canaveral—
the rocket-launching place—
a shuttle took off with a roar of fire
and headed out toward space.

Eagle had a brilliant thought
and whistled a happy tune.
"Let's hitch a trip on this rocket ship
and fly up to the moon!"

With a burst of speed the eagle flew
in the path of the rocket ship.
It took her and Armadillo aboard
and continued on its trip.

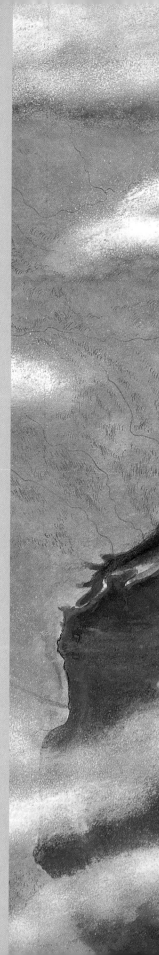

The higher they flew, the farther they saw—
Louisiana and Arkansas!
And there were some other countries below—
they could see Cuba and Mexico!

The spaceship then zoomed so high up
that Armadillo could not tell
where a country began or ended,
or where its borders fell.

The earth was now so far away—
so very, very far.
"I'm wondering," said Armadillo,
"where in the world we are."

"We're *out* of this world," said the eagle
to the armadillo, her friend.
"Ten miles from earth starts the universe
right at the atmosphere's end."

From space the earth was a big round ball,
with swirling clouds of white
against a deep-blue background,
like the blue-black sky at night.

Planets shone around them,
reflecting starlike light.
In that silent room floating in the dark,
they traveled through the night.

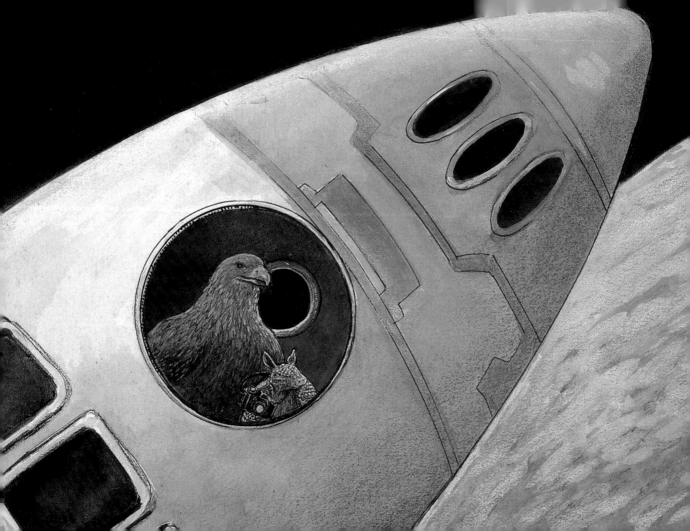

Before them was earth's silver moon—
a white and glowing sphere.
They hovered there, floating in thin air,
over craters, with no fear.

And as they watched in wonder,
the earth rose on the horizon.
They sat and gazed at their far-off home—
watched earth-set and earth-risin'.

Armadillo said, "I'm homesick.
Hey, Eagle, let's go back.
Let's go back down to our yellow town,
away from this blue and black."

The rocket began a downward arc,
then flew over land and sea.
The adventurous pair flew through the air
to their home by the yellow prairie.

He'd wondered where in the world he was,
and now Armadillo knew.
He said, "I know where, in the scheme of things,
I am, Eagle, thanks to you!

"I now live near Amarillo,
a city that's rather small,
which is in the state of Texas,
one of fifty states in all,

"in the United States of America,
the country of my birth,
on the North American continent,
in the world, on planet earth.

"In all, there are nine planets,
and earth is only one,
and as we converse, in the universe,
eight planets besides this one
warmly, hotly, coldly, coolly
revolve around the sun."

Think About It

1 Why does Armadillo go on his journey? What does he learn?

2 On the last page of the story, Armadillo tells exactly where he is. Tell exactly where you are, starting with your school.

3 The author, Lynne Cherry, used rhyming words in her story. How would the story be different if she had not?

DEAR SASPARILLO,
I'M GLAD YOU FOUND
YOUR WAY BACK TO
YOUR NEW HOME. YOUR
POSTCARDS FROM ALL
OVER THE PLACE HAVE
INSPIRED ME TO ROAM.
   LOVE,
   BRILLO

SASPARILLO ARMA
GENERAL DELIVE
AMARILLO, TX
   79 10

DEAR SASPARILLO
HELLO, DEAR COUSIN!
I'VE JUST ESCAPED FROM
THE PHILADELPHIA ZOO, AND
NOW I'M OFF TO SEE THE
WORLD FROM A DIFFERENT
CITY THAN YOU. I'M LEAVING
PHILADELPHIA, PENNSYLVANIA
IS MY STATE. WITH MY TAIL-TIP
CURLED, I'LL EXPLORE THE
WORLD! I CAN HARDLY
WAIT! LOVE, BRILLO

POST CARD

SASPARILLO ARMA
GENERAL DELIVE
AMARILLO, TX
79109

Meet the Author and Illustrator
Lynne Cherry

Lynne Cherry enjoys watching animals and nature. Her art shows the beauty she sees in life. By traveling and learning about other places authors can get new ideas. Here is a passport with more information about Lynne Cherry.

PASSPORT
Lynne Cherry

Number: J00932A09 Armadillo

Name: Lynne Cherry

Address: Washington, D.C., and Maryland

Country of birth: United States of America

Place of birth: Philadelphia, PA, U.S.A.

Date of birth: January 5, 1952

Profession: Author and Illustrator of children's picture books

Visit *The Learning Site!*
www.harcourtschool.com

Mapping the World

by Barbara Taylor

Y ou have probably seen many flat maps of the world, with the Earth's land and sea stretched out on one page or sheet. But because the Earth is round, the only really accurate map of the world is a globe—a round model of the Earth.

Globes show us the true size and shape of our land and sea. They are also tilted at a slight angle because the Earth leans slightly to one side. But globes are hard to carry around. They cannot be folded up and put in a pocket like a flat map, so we use flat maps more often.

Old Maps

Hundreds of years ago most people believed that the Earth was flat, like a giant tabletop. They thought they would fall off the edge if they sailed far enough out to sea. This map was drawn about 500 years ago. Although it is not accurate, it is easy to recognize the shapes of the different land areas. Can you recognize parts of Europe and Africa?

Try This!

Have you ever had to wrap up a round birthday present? Try covering a ball with a single sheet of paper and not leaving any gaps. You can see how hard it is to make a flat map of the Earth.

Think About It

When is a flat map better than a globe?

Response Activities

Travel Plan

MAKE A TRAVEL GUIDE

Armadillo's cousin Brillo decides to travel and explore, too. Choose a state for Brillo to visit. Look in the encyclopedia or on the Internet for information about that state. Then write a travel guide that tells Brillo what he should see and do there.

Alike and Different

COMPARE EXPLORERS

In "The Armadillo from Amarillo," Armadillo explores and learns about the world. Think about some famous explorers you have read about. With a partner, talk about how Armadillo is like those explorers. How is he different from them?

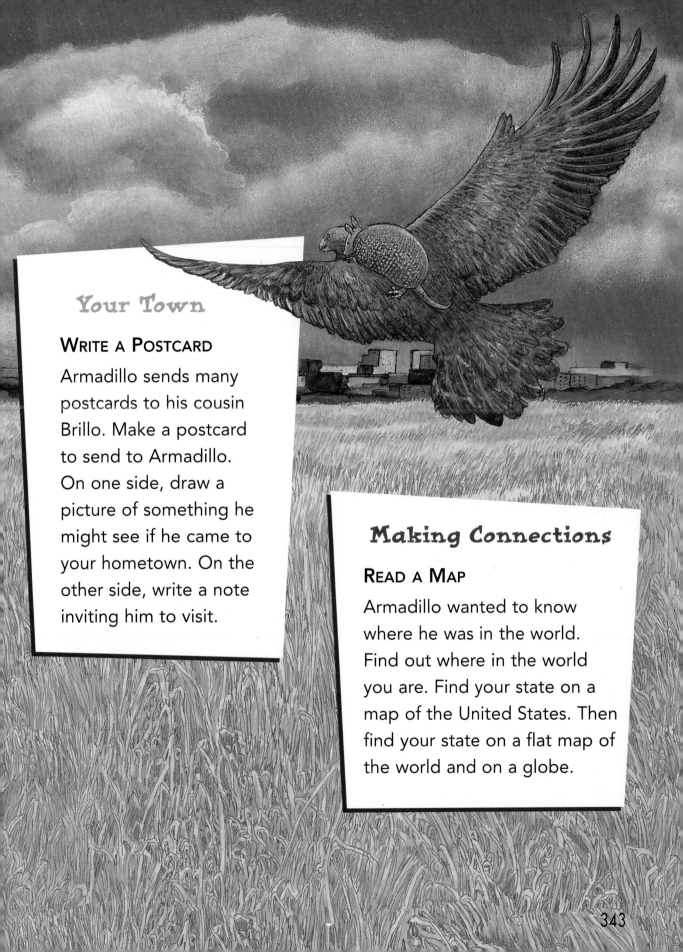

Your Town

WRITE A POSTCARD

Armadillo sends many postcards to his cousin Brillo. Make a postcard to send to Armadillo. On one side, draw a picture of something he might see if he came to your hometown. On the other side, write a note inviting him to visit.

Making Connections

READ A MAP

Armadillo wanted to know where he was in the world. Find out where in the world you are. Find your state on a map of the United States. Then find your state on a flat map of the world and on a globe.

VISITORS FROM SPACE

Award-Winning
Author

by Jeanne Bendick

illustrated by David Schleinkofer

Look!
A Comet

This is what a big, bright comet looks like in the sky.

Long ago, people thought a comet was a warning that something terrible was going to happen on Earth. It might be an earthquake, a flood, or maybe a war. Why else would a flaming ball suddenly appear in the sky?

Today we know much more about comets. A comet is not a warning of bad things to come. And we know that comets do not appear suddenly. We just don't notice them until they are near the Sun.

The Oort cloud may be like a giant shell around the Solar System.

It was named after a Dutch astronomer, Jan H. Oort.

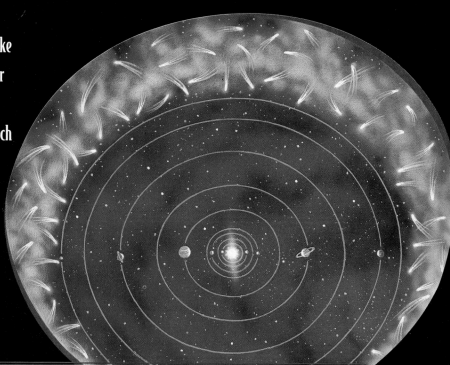

Where Do Comets Come From?

Astronomers are scientists who study the planets and stars. They think that comets are made of bits of rock, dust, ice, and gas that were left over when the *Solar System* formed about $4\frac{1}{2}$ billion years ago. The Solar System is the Sun and its family of planets and moons.

Scientists think that far out in space, out past the farthest planet from our Sun, there is a huge cloud of comets wrapped around our Solar System. There may be billions of comets there, moving around like a giant swarm of bees.

A Comet Starts Its Travels

Once in a while, some faraway star gives a sudden push or pull that can yank a comet out of the comet cloud. The comet may shoot off into space. Or it may start moving through the Solar System, toward the Sun.

Everything in the Solar System is connected to the Sun by a force you cannot see. This force is called *gravity*.

The Sun's gravity pulls on the planets and their moons. It pulls on the flying rocks in the Solar System called the *asteroids*. It pulls on comets. It pulls them all toward the star that is the center of our Solar System. That star is our Sun.

The Sun's gravity pulls the planets inward. At the same time, the planets' own energy of motion is trying to fling them off into space. These two forces balance exactly.

Comets Change

Some comets look like fuzzy balls.

Some comets look like long-haired stars.

A comet starts out as a ball of frozen gases. One astronomer calls comets "dirty snowballs."

That dirty snowball is the *nucleus* of the comet. It is the seed around which the rest of the comet grows. It may be a big seed—a mile or even a few miles wide.

As the comet comes closer to the hot Sun, the ice begins to melt. The frozen gases spread into a misty cloud around the nucleus. That cloud is called the *coma*. The coma may be half a million miles across.

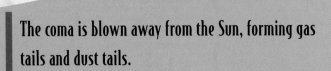

dust tail

gas tail

The coma is blown away from the Sun, forming gas tails and dust tails.

Part of the coma is pushed behind the comet. A force from the Sun called the *solar wind* blows this *tail* out behind the comet.

Most comets grow two tails or more. One tail is gas. It is straight and long—maybe 10 million miles long.

The other tails are shorter and curved. They are made of dust.

The tails of a comet always point away from the Sun. After the comet loops around the Sun, the solar wind blows the tail out in front of the comet.

Comet Glow?

Out in space, comets are dark. They have no light of their own.

As they approach the Sun they begin to glow. The icy particles reflect the sunlight.

Comets reflect sunlight even at night. Reflected sunlight also makes our Moon and the planets shine. Only stars have their own light.

Something else makes comets glow. The gas in the coma soaks up some of the sunlight. It becomes like the gas in a fluorescent light bulb. It glows.

Mars

A comet's orbit is
usually an ellipse.

354

About Orbits

The planets move around the Sun in regular paths, called *orbits*. The orbit of a planet is almost round. When a planet orbits the Sun once, it is a *year* on that planet.

Comets also move in orbits around the Sun. Their orbits are shaped more like eggs. These orbits are called *ellipses* [i · lip′ sēz]. Comet orbits may be really long, if the comet starts far out in space.

Some comets take thousands or even millions of years to complete their orbits. Other comets take only a few years. Their orbits might crisscross the orbits of the planets. The time it takes a comet to complete its orbit is called the comet's *period*.

Comets move fast. But they seem to almost stand still in the sky for many nights in a row. They do not seem to move because they are so far away. Doesn't the Moon seem to stand still, too? You have to watch it for a long time to see that it is moving.

The Most
Famous Comet

Certain comets appear in the sky again and again. We can predict when they will come. These comets are usually given names. Comets are usually named for the people who saw them first.

The most famous comet is called Halley's Comet. We see it about every 76 years, when it comes closest to the Sun. Its period is 76 years.

Halley's Comet passed us in 1985–86. It will come again in 2060. How old will you be then?

Think About It

1. How are comets different from planets?

2. What is the most interesting fact you learned about comets?

3. If you could talk with the author, what question would you ask her? Tell why you would ask that question.

Meet the Author

Jeanne Bendick

I have written many, many books. A list of my book titles would stretch on for two or three pages. Most of them are beginning books on science for young readers.

I am not a scientist, though. I am a writer who enjoys learning about a difficult science topic. First, I try to explain a new topic in simple words so that I can understand it. Then, I feel I can write about it for young people.

Through my books, I hope readers will see that science is part of everyday life. I also hope my books will make children ask questions and try to find answers. I think questions are more important than answers. Curiosity about our world is wonderful!

**Visit *The Learning Site!*
www.harcourtschool.com**

Response

DOCTOR COMET

DRAW A DIAGRAM

Make a diagram of a comet and label the parts. Use facts from the selection to help you. Then imagine that you are a scientist visiting your class. Show your diagram, and tell everything you know about comets.

LIGHT SHOW

WRITE A POEM

Imagine that you have seen a comet, and write a poem that tells what it looked like. Use facts in the selection or from another source to help you. Read your poem to your classmates.

Activities

ORBIT WALK

MODEL THE SOLAR SYSTEM

Work in a group of ten to show how the planets in our solar system go around the Sun. One person can be the Sun, and the others can be the nine planets. Then the "planets" can walk slowly around the "Sun" to show the orbits.

SPACE SCIENTISTS

WRITE A BIOGRAPHY

Look in an encyclopedia or a science book for information about a famous astronomer, such as Maria Mitchell or Edmund Halley. Write a short report about this person. Read your report to your classmates.

Theme Wrap-Up

360

Exploration Mural

DRAW A MURAL Work in a group to make a mural about exploring our world, from the core of the earth right out into space. Decide how the selections connect to this theme by choosing ideas from them that can be shown in drawings. Then your group can use markers, crayons, or paint to add color.

Splash Poem

WRITE A POEM A splash poem is made up of words and phrases that remind you of a certain topic. The words are written in any place or order on a sheet of paper. Choose words and phrases from selections in this theme. Write them splashed, or scattered, on your paper. Draw a picture to go with your poem.

What's the Connection?

MAKE A THEME WEB All of the selections in this theme are related to the idea "Celebrate Our World." Some selections are also connected to other selections by similar ideas. Make a web that shows how all these selections are connected. Your web may look like the one shown here. Add other stories you have read that might fit in this theme.

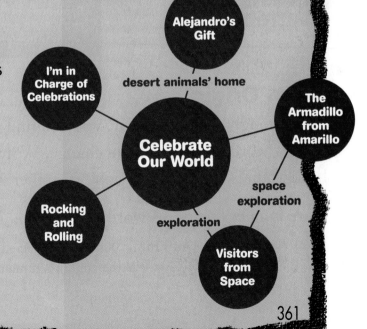

Using the Glossary

Like a dictionary, this glossary lists words in alphabetical order. To find a word, look it up by its first letter or letters.

To save time, use the **guide words** at the top of each page. These show you the first and last words on the page. Look at the guide words to see if your word falls between them alphabetically.

Here is an example of a glossary entry:

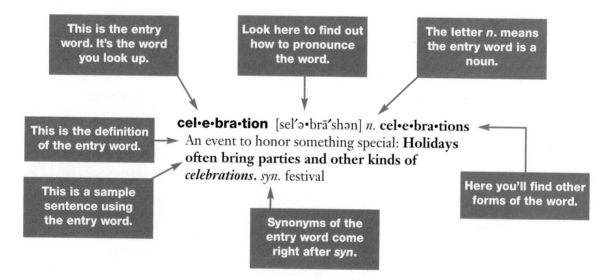

This is the entry word. It's the word you look up.

Look here to find out how to pronounce the word.

The letter *n.* means the entry word is a noun.

This is the definition of the entry word.

This is a sample sentence using the entry word.

cel•e•bra•tion [sel′ə•brā′shən] *n.* **cel•e•bra•tions**
An event to honor something special: **Holidays often bring parties and other kinds of** *celebrations.* *syn.* festival

Synonyms of the entry word come right after *syn.*

Here you'll find other forms of the word.

Word Origins

Throughout the glossary, you will find notes about word origins, or how words get started and change. Words often have interesting backgrounds that can help you remember what they mean.

Here is an example of a word origin note:

harvest Until the 1700s, *harvest* named the season we now know as *autumn*. That was the time when many crops were picked.

Pronunciation

The pronunciation in brackets is a respelling that shows how the word is pronounced.

The **pronunciation key** explains what the symbols in a respelling mean. A shortened pronunciation key appears on every other page of the glossary.

PRONUNCIATION KEY*

a	add, map	m	move, seem	u	up, done
ā	ace, rate	n	nice, tin	û(r)	burn, term
â(r)	care, air	ng	ring, song	yoo	fuse, few
ä	palm, father	o	odd, hot	v	vain, eve
b	bat, rub	ō	open, so	w	win, away
ch	check, catch	ô	order, jaw	y	yet, yearn
d	dog, rod	oi	oil, boy	z	zest, muse
e	end, pet	ou	pout, now	zh	vision, pleasure
ē	equal, tree	oŏ	took, full	ə	the schwa, an
f	fit, half	oo	pool, food		unstressed vowel
g	go, log	p	pit, stop		representing the
h	hope, hate	r	run, poor		sound spelled
i	it, give	s	see, pass		*a* in *above*
ī	ice, write	sh	sure, rush		*e* in *sicken*
j	joy, ledge	t	talk, sit		*i* in *possible*
k	cool, take	th	thin, both		*o* in *melon*
l	look, rule	th	this, bathe		*u* in *circus*

Other symbols
- separates words into syllables
- ′ indicates heavier stress on a syllable
- ′ indicates light stress on a syllable

Abbreviations: *adj.* adjective, *adv.* adverb, *conj.* conjunction, *interj.* interjection, *n.* noun, *prep.* preposition, *pron.* pronoun, *syn.* synonym, *v.* verb

* The Pronunciation Key, adapted entries, and the Short Key that appear on the following pages are reprinted from *HBJ School Dictionary* Copyright © 1990 by Harcourt Brace & Company. Reprinted by permission of Harcourt Brace & Company.

a·ban·don [ə·ban′dən] *v.* To leave behind: **When the car broke down, the travelers had to *abandon* it and walk.**

ad·vice [ad·vīs′] *n.* Suggestions or directions on what to do: **Tom asked for *advice* on how to set up his computer.**

a·mount [ə·mount′] *n.* A certain number of: **We saved our money in the bank until we had the *amount* we needed for our trip.** *syn.* quantity

> **Word Origins**
>
> **amount** *Amount* comes from the Latin *ad montem*, which means "to the mountain," and so "going in an upward direction." As you add up numbers to find the amount, or sum, you are "climbing a mountain" of numbers!

am·ple [am′pəl] *adj.* Enough or more than enough: **We had *ample* food for everyone, so no one went hungry.**

ar·range [ə·rānj′] *v.* **ar·ranged** To place things in a certain order: **Lian *arranged* the books on the shelf from tallest to shortest.** *syn.* organize

auc·tion·eer [ôk′shən·ir′] *n.* A person who sells things at a public sale to people offering the highest prices: **The *auctioneer* spoke very fast as he called out the prices being offered.**

av·er·age [av′rij] *adj.* Usual or ordinary: **Juan is an *average* runner, not unusually fast or slow.**

bar·gain [bär′gən] *v.* To work out an agreement about selling or trading something: **Mother had to *bargain* with our neighbor to trade some of our corn for some of his eggs.**

bid [bid] *n.* An offer to pay a certain price for something: **Sally wanted to buy the lamp, so she made a *bid* of five dollars for it.**

bloom [blo͞om] *v.* **blooms** To open as a flower does: **A little rosebud *blooms* into a beautiful rose.**

budge [buj] *v.* To move even a little bit: **We pushed and pulled with all our might, but we could not *budge* the heavy rock.**

can·yon [kan′yən] *n.* A deep valley with high cliffs on both sides: **When you look down into a *canyon*, you may see a river running through it.**

canyon

ca·reer [kə·rir′] *n.* The kind of work a person does in his or her life: **Rosita had to decide between a *career* as a doctor or as a dancer.** *syns.* profession, occupation

cel·e·bra·tion [sel′ə·brā′shən] *n.*
cel·e·bra·tions An event to honor
something special: **Holidays often bring
parties and other kinds of *celebrations*.**
syn. festival

cher·ish [cher′ish] *v.* **cher·ished** To care
about or hold dear: **Helga *cherished* the
doll her grandmother had given her.**

choice [chois] *n.* **choic·es** What you decide
to have or to do: **When you decide what
you want to eat and to wear, you are
making *choices*.** *syn.* selection

choos·y [chōō′zē] *adj.* Very careful about
deciding; paying close attention to: **Joan is
choosy about what she wears, so it takes
her a long time to dress.** *syn.* fussy

clutch [kluch] *v.* **clutched** To hold onto
something tightly: **Larisa *clutched* her
purse in both hands on the crowded bus.**
syn. grasp

coast [kōst] *n.* Land that is along the sea:
**Cities along the *coast* can be reached by
ship as well as by train.** *syn.* seashore

Word Origins

coast What does a rib have to do
with a coast? In Latin, *costa* means
"rib," and people in the past used
coast to mean "side." People now use
coast to mean "seashore" or "seaside"
because we think of the coast as
being the land at the "side" or
"edge" of the ocean.

---

com·bi·na·tion [kom′bə·nā′shən] *n.*
com·bi·na·tions Something made by
putting other things together: **Salads
usually are *combinations* of different
kinds of vegetables or fruits.**

con·grat·u·la·tions [kən·grach′ə·lā′shənz]
n. Good wishes to someone who has done
well: **When our team won the game, the
coach gave us his *congratulations*.**

con·ti·nent
[kon′tə·nənt] *n.*
One of the main
areas of land that
make up the earth:
**The United States
is part of the
continent of North
America.**

continent

cor·ral [kə·ral′] *n.* A fenced-in space for
farm animals: **The cattle were put in a
corral to keep them from wandering
away.** *syn.* pen

coun·cil [koun′səl] *n.* A group of people
who meet to talk about something or
to make plans: **The *council* met, and
members decided to clean up the park.**

Fact File

council A city *council* is a group of
men and women who are chosen by
the people of the city. They make
laws that help the city run smoothly.
The American colonies modeled
their first city governments after
those in England.

---

a add	e end	o odd	ōō pool	oi oil	th this		*a* in *above*
ā ace	ē equal	ō open	u up	ou pout	zh vision		*e* in *sicken*
â care	i it	ô order	û burn	ng ring		ə =	*i* in *possible*
ä palm	ī ice	ōō took	yōō fuse	th thin			*o* in *melon*
							u in *circus*

365

coun·ty [koun′tē] *n.* One of the parts into which a state is divided: **My uncle lives in the same state as I do, but in a different** *county*.

county

cous·in [kuz′(ə)n] *n.* **cous·ins** A person or animal that is related to another person or animal but is not closely related: **The wolf and jackal are** *cousins* **of the dog.** *syns.* relative, kin

dam·age [dam′ij] *v.* **dam·aged** To harm something so that it is not as good as it was before: **The radio was** *damaged* **when someone left it out in the rain.**

dread·ful [dred′fəl] *adj.* Awful; very bad: **The** *dreadful* **tornado struck the town with a roar.** *syns.* terrible, fearful

driz·zle [driz′əl] *n.* A very light rain: **The rain changed to a light** *drizzle* **and soon stopped.**

du·ty [d(y)oo′tē] *n.* Something that should be done because it is right or important: **Police officers have a** *duty* **to keep people safe.**

earn [ûrn] *v.* **earned** To make money by doing work: **My brothers** *earned* **money for their trip by mowing lawns and raking leaves.**

edge [ej] *n.* **edg·es** The line where a thing begins or ends: **Tomeka put the dishes near the** *edges* **of the table to make room for the turkey.**

edges

ed·i·tor [ed′i·tər] *n.* A person who may make changes to a writer's work to get it ready to be published: **A good** *editor* **can help make a writer's work even better.**

en·tire [in·tīr′] *adj.* Including everything; with nothing missing: **Be sure to paint the** *entire* **chair, not just the parts on top that you can see.** *syns.* whole, complete

ep·i·cen·ter [ep′i·sen′tər] *n.* The place on the earth's surface that is right above the point where an earthquake begins: **Scientists said that the** *epicenter* **of the earthquake was five miles south of the city.**

e·ven·tu·al·ly [i·ven′choo·əl·ē] *adv.* Over time; in the end: **At first the kitten was afraid, but** *eventually* **it learned to trust us.** *syn.* finally

fare [fâr] **far·ing** *v.* To get along; to do; to manage: **We were** *faring* **just fine on our nature walk until a skunk crossed our path.**

fare·well [fâr·wel′] *n.* Words spoken when leaving; a good-bye: **As Teresa was leaving, she told her friends** *farewell*.

feast [fēst] *n.* A special meal with a large amount of food: **The king gave a great** *feast* **to celebrate his daughter's wedding.** *syn.* banquet

fluo·res·cent [floo·res′ənt] *adj.* Describes something that gives off cool light: **Some** *fluorescent* **lightbulbs are in the shape of long, white tubes.**

force [fôrs] *n.* Power or energy to cause something to move or to stop moving: **A sailboat uses the** *force* **of the wind to move across the water.** *syn.* strength

for·tune [fôr′chən] *n.* **for·tunes** What may happen to someone in the future; a person's path to success: **Van and his friends hoped to find their** *fortunes* **as they boarded the ship to a faraway land.** *syn.* luck

fur·row [fûr′ō] *n.* **fur·rows** A long groove or cut made in the ground by a plow or another tool: **The farmer plowed neat** *furrows* **in the soil and planted the seeds in them.**

furrows

gal·lop [gal′əp] *v.* **gal·loped** To ride a horse that is running fast: **Henry was in a hurry to get home, so he got on his horse and** *galloped* **across the field.**

gaze [gāz] *v.* **gaz·ing** To look at something in a way that shows great interest or wonder: **Jamal spent hours** *gazing* **at the clouds as they moved and changed.** *syn.* stare

glis·ten [glis′(ə)n] *v.* **glis·tened** To shine or sparkle: **The lake** *glistened* **in the sunshine.**

growth [grōth] *n.* Plants or things that become greater in size and number in a certain place: **There was a** *growth* **of weeds around the empty house.**

grum·ble [grum′bəl] *v.* **grum·bling** To complain in a low voice and in an angry or unhappy way: **Bert kept** *grumbling* **all day because he couldn't go out to play.** *syn.* mutter

H

har·vest [här′vist] *v.* To pick or gather a crop, such as grain, fruits, or vegetables: **When the apples are ripe, it's time to** *harvest* **them.**

Word Origins

harvest Until the 1700s, *harvest* named the season we now know as *autumn*. That was the time when many crops were picked.

home·ward [hōm′wərd] *adv.* Toward home: **After we walked to the pond and fed the ducks, we turned** *homeward*.

a add	e end	o odd	o͞o pool	oi oil	th this	a in *above*
ā ace	ē equal	ō open	u up	ou pout	zh vision	e in *sicken*
â care	i it	ô order	û burn	ng ring		ə = { i in *possible*
ä palm	ī ice	o͝o took	yo͞o fuse	th thin		o in *melon*
						u in *circus*

in·vis·i·ble [in·viz′ə·bəl] *adj.* Not able to be seen: **Air is all around us, but we can't see it because it is *invisible*.**

loop [lo͞op] *v.* **loops** To move in a circle or an oval: **The plane leaves a white trail as it *loops* across the sky.**

loops

ma·chet·e [mə·shet′ē *or* mə·shet′] *n.* A large knife with a heavy blade, often used as a tool, especially in Latin American countries: **Manuel uses a *machete* to cut sugarcane in the fields.**

mag·ma [mag′mə] *n.* Very hot, partly melted rock inside the earth: **Can you imagine how hot it must be inside the earth to melt rocks into *magma*?**

mar·ket [mär′kit] *n.* A place where goods are sold: **After the peaches are picked, trucks take them to the *market* to be sold.**

mis·chief [mis′chif] *n.* Action that is naughty or that may cause harm: **My mother has to watch my younger brother all the time to keep him out of *mischief*.**

ne·ces·si·ty [nə·ses′ə·tē] *n.* **ne·ces·si·ties** Something that is needed: **Food and water are two of the *necessities* of life.**

non·sense [non′sens′] *n.* Something that is silly or that does not make sense: **The story about pigs flying is *nonsense*.** *syn.* foolishness

nu·cle·us [n(y)o͞o′klē·əs] *n.* The center of something: **The pit is the *nucleus* of a peach.**

par·ti·cle [pär′ti·kəl] *n.* **par·ti·cles** A very tiny bit of something: **Did you know that grains of sand are really *particles* of broken rock?**

peak [pēk] *n.* The pointed top of a hill or mountain: **This mountain *peak* is so high that there is always snow on it, even in summer.**

peak

per·fect [pər·fekt′] *v.* To make something as good as it can be: **Micah practiced every day, trying to *perfect* his speech for the school assembly.**

por·tion [pôr′shən] *n.* **por·tions** The amount of something given to one person; part of a whole: **I ate two *portions* of mashed potatoes last night.**

pride [prīd] *n.* A feeling of being proud of or having respect for; a feeling of worth: **We keep our streets clean and safe because we have *pride* in our city.**

prof·it [prof′it] *n.* Money gained by selling something: **After Carlos and Isabel paid for the lemons and sugar, they found that they hadn't made much *profit* from selling lemonade.**

pulp [pulp] *n.* The soft, juicy inside of some fruits and vegetables: **Eat the *pulp* of the melon, not the skin.**

ranch·er [ran′chər] *n.* **ranchers** A person who owns a large farm for raising animals, such as cattle, sheep, or horses: ***Ranchers* need a lot of land so that their animals will have enough grass to eat.**

range [rānj] *n.* A row or line of mountains: **The mountain *range* looks small on the map, but it is long in real life.**

range

re·ceive [ri•sēv′] *v.* To get something: **I like to give gifts, and I like to *receive* them, too.**

re·tell·er [rē•tel′ər] *n.* A person who tells a story again, often in a new way: **Grandfather is a good *reteller* of stories he heard when he was a boy.**

Fact File

retelling *Folktales* are stories that are passed down through time. Long ago, most folktales were spoken. As people retold folktales, they often changed them a little. The Cinderella story is told in more than a thousand different ways around the world.

sat·is·fy [sat′is•fī] *v.* **sat·is·fied** To meet someone's needs or wishes: **Dawn kept changing her picture until she was *satisfied* with the way it looked.** *syn.* please

schoon·er [skoo′nər] *n.* A sailing ship that has two or more masts, or poles, that hold up the sails: **We saw a model of an old-fashioned *schooner* at the ship museum.**

schooner

a	add	e	end	o	odd	o͞o	pool	oi	oil	th	this	ə =	*a* in *above*
ā	ace	ē	equal	ō	open	u	up	ou	pout	zh	vision		*e* in *sicken*
â	care	i	it	ô	order	û	burn	ng	ring				*i* in *possible*
ä	palm	ī	ice	o͝o	took	y͞oo	fuse	th	thin				*o* in *melon*
													u in *circus*

shun [shun] *v.* **shunned** To stay away from: **The duckling was *shunned* by the mother hen and her chicks.** *syn.* avoid

sig·nal [sig′nəl] *v.* To use an action, symbol, or an object to send a message or to make something known: **We tied balloons to our mailbox to *signal* my sister's birthday.**

skill·ful [skil′fəl] *adj.* Having the ability to do something very well: **Mr. Green is a *skillful* carpenter who knows how to build fine houses.**

so·lar wind [sō′lər wind] *n.* A flow of gases or particles given off by the sun: **The *solar wind* is different from the kind of wind we have on Earth.**

> ┌ **Fact File**
> **solar wind** On Earth, hurricane winds can have speeds of 100 miles per hour. In space, the speed of *solar wind* is about 310 miles per *second!* However, the earth's magnetic forces stop particles in the solar wind from reaching the earth.

sphere [sfir] *n.* An object that has a shape like a ball: **A baseball is a small *sphere*, and a beach ball is a larger one.** *syn.,* globe

sprawl [sprôl] *v.* **sprawled** To sit or lie with the arms and legs spread out: **Jimmy *sprawled* in his seat until his mom told him to sit up straight.**

sprawled

stray [strā] *adj.* Wandering or lost: **We helped the *stray* dog find its way home.**

suc·cess [sək·ses′] *n.* Getting what one has worked for: **After many years of hard work, Antonio finally gained *success* as an artist.**

sum·mons [sum′ənz] *n.* An order for someone to be at a certain place at a certain time: **The police officer gave the driver who was speeding a *summons* to traffic court.**

sup·ply [sə·plī′] *v.* **sup·plied** To give what is needed: **Our garden *supplied* all the vegetables we could eat.** *syn.* provide

> ┌ **Word Origins**
> **supply** *Supply* comes from the Latin *supplēre*, which means "to fill up" or "to complete." We use it to mean "provide" because a supply is used to fill a need.

sup·port [sə·pôrt′] *v.* To hold the weight of something or someone: **The old wooden bridge isn't strong enough to *support* a car.**

sus·pi·cious [sə·spish′əs] *adj.* Not trusting: **We were *suspicious* of the stranger, so we stayed away from him.** *syn.* doubtful

swift·ly [swift′lē] *adv.* In a very fast way: **The jet moved *swiftly* across the sky.** *syns.* quickly, rapidly

tend [tend] *v.* **tend·ing** To take care of: **The mother bird was busy *tending* her babies.**

track [trak] *n.* **tracks** Footprints or other marks left by a person, an animal, or a thing: **We could see from the *tracks* in the mud that a deer had walked there.**

trad·ing [trā′ding] *adj.* Having to do with exchanging goods: **A *trading* post was a place where hunters sold animal skins and bought things they needed.**

tum·ble·weed [tum′bəl·wēd′] *n.* **tum·ble·weeds** A kind of bushy plant that dries up and then rolls across the ground when the wind blows: **The wind had blown *tumbleweeds* against the fence.**

tumbleweeds

un·e·vent·ful·ly [un′i·vent′fəl·ē] *adv.* With no special or unusual things happening: **After the big storm on Monday, Tuesday went by quietly and *uneventfully*.**

u·ni·verse [yōō′nə·vûrs′] *n.* Everything that is, including the Earth, the sun, planets, stars, and all of space: **Earth is like a tiny dot compared to the size of the *universe*.**

Word Origins
Universe comes from *universus*, the Latin word for "whole" or "entire."

val·ue [val′yōō] *n.* How much something is worth: **Even though a dime is smaller in size than a nickel, the dime has a greater *value*.** *syn.* worth

var·y [vâr′ē] *v.* **var·ied** To make different: **Instead of playing the same games all the time, we *varied* them from day to day.** *syn.* change

wail [wāl] *v.* **wail·ing** To cry: **The baby was *wailing* to be fed.**

wind·mill [wind′mil′] *n.* A machine that uses the power of the wind to grind grain, pump water, or do other work: **As the wind blew, the long blades of the *windmill* turned around and around.**

windmill

wits [wits] *n. (pl.)* The ability to think; good sense: **I needed my *wits* about me to find my way home in the snowstorm.**

a add	e end	o odd	o͞o pool	oi oil	t͟h this	*a* in *above*
ā ace	ē equal	ō open	u up	ou pout	zh vision	*e* in *sicken*
â care	i it	ô order	û burn	ng ring		ə = *i* in *possible*
ä palm	ī ice	o͝o took	yōō fuse	th thin		*o* in *melon*
						u in *circus*

Index of Titles

Page numbers in color refer to biographical information.

Acknowledgments

For permission to reprint copyrighted material, grateful acknowledgment is made to the following sources:

Atheneum Books for Young Readers, Simon & Schuster Children's Publishing Division: Cover illustration by Leonid Gore from *The Malachite Palace* by Alma Flor Ada. Illustration copyright © 1998 by Leonid Gore. *Cloudy With a Chance of Meatballs* by Judi Barrett, illustrated by Ron Barrett. Text copyright © 1978 by Judi Barrett; illustrations copyright © 1978 by Ron Barrett. *I'm in Charge of Celebrations* by Byrd Baylor, illustrated by Peter Parnall. Text copyright © 1986 by Byrd Baylor; illustrations copyright © 1986 by Peter Parnall. Cover illustration by Robert Roth from *mama provi and the pot of rice* by Sylvia Rosa-Casanova. Illustration copyright © 1997 by Robert Roth.

Boyds Mills Press, Inc.: *Leah's Pony* by Elizabeth Friedrich, illustrated by Michael Garland. Text copyright © 1996 by Elizabeth Friedrich; illustrations copyright © 1996 by Michael Garland.

Curtis Brown, Ltd: Corrected galley from *Borreguita and the Coyote* by Verna Aardema. Text copyright © 1992 by Verna Aardema. Originally published in *A Bookworm Who Hatched,* Richard C. Owen Publishers, Inc., 1993.

Candlewick Press, Cambridge, MA: From *Rocking and Rolling* by Phillip Steele. Text copyright © 1997 by Phillip Steele; illustrations copyright © 1997 by Walker Books Ltd.

Carolrhoda Books, Inc., Minneapolis, MN: Cover illustration by Peter J. Thornton from *Everybody Bakes Bread* by Norah Dooley. Copyright 1996 by Carolrhoda Books, Inc. Cover photograph by Bob Firth from *Farms Feed the World* by Lee Sullivan Hill. Copyright 1997 by Carolrhoda Books, Inc.

Chronicle Books: *Alejandro's Gift* by Richard E. Albert, illustrated by Sylvia Long. Text copyright © 1994 by Richard E. Albert; illustrations copyright © 1994 by Sylvia Long.

Clarion Books/Houghton Mifflin Company: Cover illustration from *What Do Authors Do?* by Eileen Christelow. Copyright © 1995 by Eileen Christelow.

Dial Books for Young Readers, a division of Penguin Putnam, Inc.: *Why Mosquitoes Buzz in People's Ears: A West African Tale,* retold by Verna Aardema, illustrated by Leo and Diane Dillon. Text copyright © 1975 by Verna Aardema; illustrations copyright © 1975 by Leo and Diane Dillon. Cover illustration by Bryna Waldman from *Anansi Finds a Fool* by Verna Aardema. Illustration copyright © 1992 by Bryna Waldman.

Farrar, Straus & Giroux, Inc.: Cover illustration from *Archibald Frisby* by Michael Chesworth. Copyright © 1994 by Michael Chesworth.

Harcourt, Inc.: *The Armadillo from Amarillo* by Lynne Cherry. Copyright © 1994 by Lynne Cherry. Stamp designs copyright © by United States Postal Service. Reproduction of images courtesy of Gilbert Palmer, the National Aeronautics and Space Administration, the Austin News Agency, Festive Enterprises, Jack Lewis/Texas Department of Transportation, the Baxter Lane Company, Wyco Colour Productions, Frank Burd, and City Sights. Cover illustration from *Water Dance* by Thomas Locker. Copyright © 1997 by Thomas Locker. *Worksong* by Gary Paulsen, illustrated by Ruth Wright Paulsen. Text copyright © 1997 by Gary Paulsen; illustrations copyright © 1997 by Ruth Wright Paulsen.

HarperCollins Publishers: Cover illustration from *Fire! Fire!* by Gail Gibbons. Copyright © 1984 by Gail Gibbons.

Houghton Mifflin Company: Cover illustration by Blair Lent from *The Wave* by Margaret Hodges. Illustration copyright © 1964 by Blair Lent.

Alfred A. Knopf, Inc.: Illustration by Petra Mathers from *Borreguita and the Coyote* by Verna Aardema. Illustration copyright © 1991 by Petra Mathers.

Larousse Kingfisher Chambers, Inc., New York: From "Mapping the World" in *Young Discoverers: Maps and Mapping* by Barbara Taylor, cover illustration by Kevin Maddison. Text and cover illustration copyright © 1992 by Grisewood and Dempsey Ltd.

Little, Brown and Company: *Yippee-Yay! A Book About Cowboys and Cowgirls* by Gail Gibbons. Copyright © 1998 by Gail Gibbons.

Lothrop, Lee & Shepard Books, a division of William Morrow & Company, Inc.: *If You Made a Million* by David M. Schwartz, illustrated by Steven Kellogg, photographs of money by George Ancona. Text copyright © 1989 by David M. Schwartz; illustrations copyright © 1989 by Steven Kellogg; photographs of money copyright © 1989 by George Ancona.

Ludlow Music, Inc., New York, NY: "This Land Is Your Land," words and music by Woody Guthrie. TRO-©-copyright 1956 (Renewed) 1958 (Renewed) and 1970 (Renewed) by Ludlow Music, Inc.

The Millbrook Press: From *Comets and Meteors: Visitors from Space* (Retitled: "Visitors from Space") by Jeanne Bendick, cover illustration by Mike Roffe. Text © 1991 by Jeanne Bendick; cover illustration © 1991 by Eagle Books Limited.

Morrow Junior Books, a division of William Morrow and Company, Inc.: "The Ant and the Dove" from *Androcles and the Lion and Other Aesop's Fables,* retold in verse by Tom Paxton, cover illustration by Robert Rayevsky. Text copyright © 1991 by Tom Paxton; cover illustration copyright © 1991 by Robert Rayevsky .

Northland Publishing Company, Flagstaff, AZ: *The Three Little Javelinas* by Susan Lowell, illustrated by Jim Harris. Text copyright © 1992 by Susan Lowell; illustrations copyright © 1992 by Jim Harris. Cover illustration by Jim Harris from *The Tortoise and the Jackrabbit* by Susan Lowell. Illustration copyright © 1994 by Jim Harris.

Orchard Books, New York: *Cocoa Ice* by Diana Appelbaum, illustrated by Holly Meade. Text © 1997 by Diana Appelbaum; illustrations © 1997 by Holly Meade.

Richard C. Owen Publishers, Inc., Katonah, NY 10536: *A Bookworm Who Hatched* by Verna Aardema, photographs by Dede Smith. Text © 1992 by Verna Aardema; photographs © 1992 by Dede Smith.

Plays, Inc.: *The Crowded House* by Eva Jacob from PLAYS: *The Drama Magazine for Young People.* Text copyright © 1959, 1970 by Plays, Inc. This play is for reading purposes only; for permission to produce, write to Plays, Inc., 120 Boylston St., Boston, MA 02116.

G.P. Putnam's Sons, a division of Penguin Putnam Inc.: Cover illustration by Susan Gaber from *Jordi's Star* by Alma Flor Ada. Illustration copyright © 1996 by Susan Gaber.

Simon & Schuster Books for Young Readers, Simon & Schuster Children's Publishing Division: Cover illustration by Floyd Cooper from *Papa Tells Chita a Story* by Elizabeth Fitzgerald Howard. Illustration copyright © 1995 by Floyd Cooper. Cover photograph from *Earth: Our Planet In Space* by Seymour Simon. Photograph courtesy of NASA. *Coyote Places the Stars* by Harriet Peck Taylor. Copyright © 1993 by Harriet Peck Taylor.

Viking Children's Books, a division of Penguin Putnam, Inc.: Cover illustration by Susanna Natti from *Cam Jansen and the Triceratops Pops Mystery* by David A. Adler. Illustration copyright © 1995 by Susanna Natti.

Photo Credits

Key: (t)=top, (b)=bottom, (c)=center, (l)=left, (r)=right (child), Verna Aardema, 60; (house), Verna Aardema, 61; Verna Aardema, 62(tr); Verna Aardema, 63(c); Verna Aardema, 65(c); Verna Aardema, 66(t); Will Hildebrand, 68; Ross Humphries, 156; Davis Photography, 157; Photo © National Gallery of Art, Washington DC, 294; courtesy, Walker Books 313, NASA, 340; The Granger Collection, New York, 341(t); Richard A. Cooke III/Tony Stone Images, 365; Ed Degginger/Bruce Coleman, Inc., 366(r); D.R. Stocklein/The Stock Market, 367(l); Michael Levine/The Picture Cube, 367(r); Jeffry W. Myers/The Stock Market, 371.

All other photos by Harcourt, Inc.

Brian Payne/Black Star, Tom Sobolik/Black Star, Walt Chrynwski/Black Star, Rick Friedman/Black Star, Alan Orling/Black Star, Gill Kenney/Black Star, John Troha/Black Star, Dale Higgins, Ken Kenzie.

Illustration Credits

Mark Buehner, Cover Art; Jennie Oppenheimer, 2-3, 10-11, 12-13, 116-117; Paul Cox, 4-5, 118-119, 120-121, 250-251; Dave LeFleur, 6-7, 252-253, 254-255, 360-361; Harriet Peck Taylor, 14-27, 28-29; Leo and Diane Dillon, 32-55, 58-59; David Galchutt, 56-57; Billy Davis, 74-75; Ron Barrett, 76-91, 92-93; Holly Cooper, 94-109, 114-115; Allen Eitzen, 110-113; Michael Garland, 122-137, 138-139; Katy Farmer, 140-141; Jim Harris, 142-157, 158-159; Holly Meade, 160-191, 192-193; Tuko Fujisaki, 194-195, 368-370; Gail Gibbons, 196-213, 216-217; Ruth Wright Paulsen, 214; Steven Kellogg, 218-245, 248-249; Ethan Long, 246-247, 136-137, 197, 216-217; Peter Parnall, 256-273, 274-275; Sylvia Long, 278-293, 296-297; Philip Steele, 298-313, 341-315; Lynn Cherry, 318-339, 342-343; David Schleinkofer, 344-357, 358-359